"Mark Salisbury's *iLearning*, I believe, is critically important considering the age of our workforce as the 'career' employees retire. A modern business system needs to have the 'learning' built into the business system, and I believe this will define the outstanding companies in the future."
—Mark D. Dickinson, Sandia National Laboratories

"Mark Salisbury combines theories on quality, knowledge, and training with our newest technologies to develop a comprehensive plan for innovation. A must-read for anyone interested in improving productivity."
—Mark Schuetz, training professional

"In Mark Salisbury's *iLearning*, he has 'cracked the code' on emergent learning. This book provides the blueprint for organizations striving to increase employee capability and performance through knowledge."
—Roderick Spaulding, Intel Corporation

"It is almost cliché to talk about the importance of collaborating and sharing knowledge across the organization to fuel innovation. What has been missing to date is a comprehensive and sustainable method for accomplishing this. With *iLearning*, Mark Salisbury has provided managers with a step-by-step guide for leveraging organizational knowledge to gain competitive advantage."
—Robert Grassberger, Ph.D., developmental economist,
New Mexico State University

"In particular, individual knowledge workers will benefit from reading *iLearning* and applying its lessons. Besides enabling organizational learning, they will be able to transform their own careers by aligning with the book's powerful concepts."
—Terence L. Lammers, Ph.D. I am not endorsing *iLearning* on
behalf of my employer, The Boeing Company.

"*iLearning* is a well-organized book that provides a logical process with examples for organizations to identify internal strengths and best practices that can be applied to develop targeted objectives and help increase performance."
—Yolanda Padilla, aerospace education design specialist

"Mark Salisbury offers a practical model that integrates instructional design, knowledge management, collaborative development, and distributed cognition. This unique integration allows learning professionals to more successfully develop and deploy training that sustains continuous improvement and fosters innovation. This book can help managers improve efficiency, operational sustainability, and competitiveness in their organization."
—Tom King, elearning industry analyst,
Mobilemind chief consultant

About This Book

Why is this topic important?

Most organizations don't know what they know when it comes to improving their performance. The traditional way of sending workers "away" to a training session to learn what they need to know does not help organizations build on what they know. Even having workers "go away" to a distance education course that is launched from their workstation takes them too far away from the learning that is needed for their immediate work. It's becoming apparent that learning must be part of work—and that it must take place in collaboration with others as teams solve problems together. iLearning is a means for organizations to facilitate this innovative learning in a purposeful manner. Once instituted, iLearning becomes an organizational strategy for innovation.

What can you achieve with this book?

iLearning shows how to represent organizational knowledge by identifying the underlying performance objectives of knowledge work. Using performance objectives to manage their knowledge, organizations can embed training, best practices, and expert advice in their collaborative work processes. They can also use this detailed knowledge to improve their processes. However, the biggest impact for organizations that embrace iLearning is that they know what they know when they are facing new challenges. This existing knowledge becomes their most powerful fuel for innovation.

After reading this book, members of organizations will be able to bring the following benefits to their companies, agencies, nonprofit organizations, and institutions:

- Managers of knowledge workers will be able to facilitate collaborative work with innovative learning, lead interventions to enable iLearning, and strategically plan for the future.

- Training professionals will have the skills to facilitate collaborative work with innovative learning and to apply the methodologies for achieving that learning.
- Human resource professionals will be able to develop interventions to facilitate iLearning and be able to plan workforce development.
- Information technology specialists will be able to apply methodologies and deploy technologies to support iLearning in organizations.

How is this book organized?

iLearning leads readers through the necessary changes needed to become an innovative learning organization. This journey unfolds through five main themes presented in the five parts of this book. Part One describes how to facilitate collaborative work in an organization. Part Two describes how to facilitate collaborative work with innovative learning. Part Three describes the organizational interventions for creating an iLearning organization. Part Four describes how to apply the methodologies and technologies that support an iLearning organization. And Part Five tells why and how iLearning is changing our world, particularly our K–12 schooling, higher education, and global economy.

iLearning has been written with a busy audience in mind—managers of knowledge workers, training and human resource professionals, and information technology specialists. Chapters are short and use many illustrations to provide quick and easy access to concepts and to put readers in command of the details needed to implement those concepts. Entertaining, and true, real-life examples in the "expert advice" section of each chapter (derived from my radio show, *The Knowledge Worker*) help readers engage with both concepts and methods.

About Pfeiffer

Pfeiffer serves the professional development and hands-on resource needs of training and human resource practitioners and gives them products to do their jobs better. We deliver proven ideas and solutions from experts in HR development and HR management, and we offer effective and customizable tools to improve workplace performance. From novice to seasoned professional, Pfeiffer is the source you can trust to make yourself and your organization more successful.

Essential Knowledge Pfeiffer produces insightful, practical, and comprehensive materials on topics that matter the most to training and HR professionals. Our Essential Knowledge resources translate the expertise of seasoned professionals into practical, how-to guidance on critical workplace issues and problems. These resources are supported by case studies, worksheets, and job aids and are frequently supplemented with CD-ROMs, Web sites, and other means of making the content easier to read, understand, and use.

Essential Tools Pfeiffer's Essential Tools resources save time and expense by offering proven, ready-to-use materials—including exercises, activities, games, instruments, and assessments—for use during a training or team-learning event. These resources are frequently offered in looseleaf or CD-ROM format to facilitate copying and customization of the material.

Pfeiffer also recognizes the remarkable power of new technologies in expanding the reach and effectiveness of training. While e-hype has often created whizbang solutions in search of a problem, we are dedicated to bringing convenience and enhancements to proven training solutions. All our e-tools comply with rigorous functionality standards. The most appropriate technology wrapped around essential content yields the perfect solution for today's on-the-go trainers and human resource professionals.

Pfeiffer *Essential resources for training and HR professionals*
www.pfeiffer.com

iLearning

How to Create an Innovative Learning Organization

Mark Salisbury

A Wiley Imprint
www.pfeiffer.com

Published by Pfeiffer
An Imprint of Wiley
989 Market Street, San Francisco, CA 94103-1741
www.pfeiffer.com

For additional copies/bulk purchases of this book in the U.S. please contact 800-274-4434.

Pfeiffer books and products are available through most bookstores. To contact Pfeiffer directly call our Customer Care Department within the U.S. at 800-274-4434, outside the U.S. at 317-572-3985, fax 317-572-4002, or visit www.pfeiffer.com.

Pfeiffer also publishes its books in a variety of electronic formats. Some content that appears in print may not be available in electronic books.

Acquiring Editor: Matthew Davis   Editorial Assistant: Lindsay Morton
Production Editor: Mark Karmendy/Susan Geraghty Manufacturing Supervisor: Becky Morgan

Library of Congress Cataloging-in-Publication Data

Salisbury, Mark, date.
   iLearning: how to create an innovative learning organization/ by Mark Salisbury.—1st ed.
       p.   cm.
   Includes bibliographical references and index.
   ISBN 978-0-470-29265-5 (cloth)
       1. Organizational learning.   2. Learning.   I. Title.
   HD58.82.S25   2008
   658.3'12404—dc22
                                                          2008016522

Printed in the United States of America
FIRST EDITION
HB Printing 10 9 8 7 6 5 4 3 2 1

For Joan, the love of my life

Contents

FIGURES AND TABLES

Figures

Tables

PREFACE

Most organizations don't know what they know when it comes to improving their performance. Often, earlier solutions that could be successfully adapted to a new problem are completely unknown to these organizations trying to solve the new problem. Sometimes, a similar problem and the solution to that problem are known by organizations—but many of the details are missing. Because they do not know what they know, these organizations spend a great amount of time and effort on re-creating the same solutions— many times in ways that were not as good as before. Innovation becomes difficult for these organizations because they spend so much of their time "reinventing the wheel" and have a hard time recognizing truly new and innovative solutions. In contrast, an organization that fosters innovative learning—iLearning—builds on what it knows to fuel innovation. Innovative learning in an organization begins with knowing what it knows through documented processes, instruction, examples, and expert advice that relate to the problem to be solved. With these assets, new knowledge can be collaboratively created to form a new and innovative solution in a just-in-time manner.

iLearning is like an onion—it has many layers. When you are looking at the outside layer, it's a paradigm—a way to promote innovation by bringing the best of the past together with the collaborative minds of today's workers to create the best solutions for the future. Peeling back a layer, iLearning is an organizational strategy—a way for an organization to create a window of opportunity to build on what it knows to solve problems in new and innovative ways. And at a yet deeper layer, it's a tactic—a pulling back from the process of work to focus on the knowledge of the work and growing that knowledge. Finally, at its core, iLearning is about improving individual, team, and organizational performance—it empowers individuals to maximize learning and their performance for their teams and organizations.

This analogy may seem to paint iLearning as something new and mysterious. Actually, it is neither. The term *iLearning* is short for *innovative learning*. It simply describes learning that is facilitated during collaborative work. That is, learning is supported when it is needed most—in the collaborative creation of new and unique solutions. And the ideas behind iLearning are not new. iLearning borrows concepts from performance support systems—getting the right information to the right people at the right time. It borrows from knowledge management principles—managing the life cycle of knowledge in organizations. It borrows from organizational learning—learning that creates innovation that cuts across the organization. And iLearning borrows techniques from instructional systems design—identifying the knowledge behind work and describing, in objective terms, the human performance needed to meet that work. In short, hardly anything about iLearning is new. What is new that this book is bringing to you is the information that will enable you to systematically apply these existing concepts, principles, and techniques in order to improve individual, team, and organizational learning and performance.

An iLearning organization can be realized with today's technology. However, iLearning in organizations will be accelerated through the application of new and emerging technologies. New cell phones will become personal workstations—giving workers the ability to share more information with others instantly. New media forms such as video will be used to communicate procedures, instruction, best practices, and expert advice. And 3-D virtual environments will also provide new ways for workers to communicate and share what they know. As discussed at the end of this book, these technological advances will make it easier for workers to know what the current problem is and what they did before to solve similar problems, and also easier for them to then learn together how they might better solve the current problem—and future related problems.

iLearning is not confined to business organizations. Even though not all learning can be achieved in an iLearning paradigm, this paradigm will have an impact on learning in general. (Can you imagine arriving at the Great Pyramids and then trying to look up five thousand years of Egyptian history on your cell phone?) However, as the world of work moves more and more to one in which we learn while we work, educational institutions will come under great pressure to change. Knowledge that is more factual—and easily accessed—will be deemphasized, and knowledge that is more conceptual and procedural will become the focus of educational experiences. This will mean more *authentic* learning experiences for students, in which they collaboratively create new knowledge to solve actual problems. As discussed in the last chapter of this book, this will have profound implications for K–12 education and institutions of higher education. And as also discussed in that last chapter, iLearning will have an accelerating and defining influence on the global economy. It will become one of the "fuels" for moving us to an economy where learning is collaborative among partners—and planned outcomes are new innovative products and the knowledge that created them.

This book was over twenty years in the making. It grew out of my years of experience at the Boeing Company; my years as head of Vitel, a knowledge management solutions provider; and my years of research and teaching in this area. The "application" sections of the chapters use the example of the McBoe Company[1] to show how the principles outlined in the book can be applied in a practical setting. McBoe is a mythical company, a combination of all my research and work experience. However, for the most part, what takes place in McBoe has actually taken place in various real organizations. Names and details have been changed to, as they say, protect the innocent and also to improve the value of these events as examples.

Note

1. McBoe is a fictitious name and does not refer to any actual company, living or dead.

ACKNOWLEDGMENTS

I have many people to thank for their help on this book. Jan Plass, a colleague while he was at the University of New Mexico, was a great help in conceptualizing early work on the theoretical foundations that would later support iLearning. I also wish to thank my clients for embracing the principles and ideas behind iLearning and its realization in solutions for their organizations; my graduate students for their long-suffering experiences with earlier versions of this book; and Michael Brasher, general manager of KANW, a public radio station in Albuquerque, New Mexico, for seeing the merit of broadcasting my radio show, *The Knowledge Worker* (the source of the Expert Advice section of each chapter).

I am thankful to Bob Grassberger, Chengyi Gao, and David Olson for their input to the initial ideas for the book; I offer a great deal of thanks to Kevin Brady, who took on the job of reviewing an early manuscript; and special thanks, too, to Mark Dickinson, who spent long hours with me discussing the underlying drivers of knowledge work and how they could be described in terms of performance objectives.

I wish to thank my literary agent, Jeff Herman, for all his help in bringing this book forward into the light of day; Matthew Davis, acquisitions editor for Wiley, for his willingness to take a chance on *iLearning;* and my copyeditor, Elspeth MacHattie, and production editor, Susan Geraghty.

And finally, I thank my three children for their patience in waiting for Dad to complete his day's writing before interrupting so he could partake in the finer adventures in life. And I thank my wife, Joan, for all her input around the content of this book as she read the drafts and gave me feedback—and for coping with the kids and many other things to give me the time to get the book written.

Introduction: Getting the Most from This Book

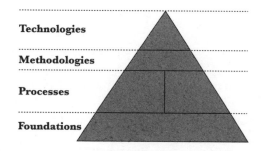

Managers of knowledge workers are bombarded with business books and consultants telling them to optimize their processes, train their people better, develop "best practices," and implement new technologies—all to improve their bottom line. With all the hype and marketing buzz, it's difficult for these managers to know which of these approaches will really improve the bottom line for their organization. Yet these managers also intuitively know that all these strategies are somehow related and are needed to improve organizational performance in the long run. That is, to really improve performance, these managers know that the people of any organization have to improve the way they work and learn together. But, how do you go about doing this? That's the challenge that managers of knowledge workers face in the early part of the twenty-first century. These managers also know that the organizations that figure it out will be the winners in the knowledge economy—and the ones that don't will be left behind. Knowing the stakes, these managers are seeking a systematic approach for improving the work and learning in their organizations. They know that if they succeed, they will reap the benefits of reducing the time to solutions, improving the quality of these solutions, and lowering the overall cost of knowledge work. They also know that success here is the key to achieving such strategic goals as merging or partnering with other organizations through outsourcing or sharing knowledge intensive processes. It's the key because once managers know what knowledge is missing in their work, then they can get it from an outside source. And the reverse is also true; once managers know what knowledge a potential partner might need, then they can bring that knowledge to the partnership.

WHO SHOULD READ THIS BOOK

iLearning is for managers of knowledge workers, training and human resource professionals, and information technology specialists. It provides them with the answer to their question about how the people in their organizations can improve working and learning together—and that answer lies in focusing on the knowledge of their organizations. *iLearning* shows how to represent organizational knowledge by identifying the underlying performance objectives of knowledge work and modeling those performance objectives and their interrelations. By going to this level of detail in modeling their knowledge, organizations can embed training, best practices, and expert advice in their processes. They can also use this detailed knowledge to improve their processes. However, the biggest impact for organizations that use performance objectives to model their knowledge is that they know what they know when they are facing new challenges. This becomes their most powerful fuel for innovation. It's a simple concept really. How can organizations innovate if they do not know how they currently do things? In the iLearning paradigm, workers involved in collaboration have access to the best thinking of the past—a process document, a little instruction, an example, and some expert advice. Knowing the *best old way* gives them the opportunity to learn and the resources to create a *better new way*—that's innovation. Not knowing the best old way delivers the curse of not learning anything new and simply reinventing that old way—making today's production more inefficient and resulting in no lessons learned for tomorrow's production.

The Organization of This Book

iLearning is organized into five main parts: Part One, "Facilitating Collaborative Work"; Part Two, "Facilitating Innovative Learning"; Part Three, "Enabling an iLearning Organization"; Part Four, "Applying Methodologies and Deploying Technologies"; and Part Five, "Future Directions for iLearning."

Part One: Facilitating Collaborative Work

Part One (Chapters One through Five) focuses on facilitating collaborative work. To facilitate collaborative work, the people in organizations have to *become one mind* about the work that is to be done. They have to agree on their workflow process. And within that process they have to define their roles or, said another way, their rules of engagement. They need to uncover the drivers of work—the performance objectives that need to be met by the work. These performance objectives are the key to improving the workflow process. They determine what to measure in order to provide feedback on how well the people in an organization are working together and how to go about making improvements in the way they work together.

Chapter One, "Why iLearning?" discusses why iLearning is needed for the next level of innovation in organizations. This chapter examines what *instructional systems design* shares with iLearning and how to gain a systemic viewpoint on organizational performance problems.

Chapter Two, "Becoming One Mind," discusses where and why the theory of distributed cognition is a good foundation for facilitating collaborative work. It also describes how to apply this theory to facilitate collaborative work in your organization.

Chapter Three, "Agreeing on the Workflow Process," discusses when a nontraditional way of defining an organization's process may work better than a traditional approach. It describes why it's difficult for people to agree on a workflow process in an organization and how to help people agree on one in your organization.

Chapter Four, "Defining the Roles Within the Process," discusses when and why defining roles within a process will improve the quality and timeliness of work. Then it describes how to do it in your organization.

Chapter Five, "Working the Process," discusses when and why measuring performance is the key to improving processes. This chapter concludes by describing how to measure performance in your organization.

Part Two: Facilitating Innovative Learning

Part Two (Chapters Six through Nine) focuses on facilitating innovative learning. It describes why organizations must first make a distinction between explicit and tacit knowledge. It also describes why workers have differing cognitive needs and how to respond to those needs by categorizing knowledge into different types. Finally, it describes how to develop knowledge assets that provide access to the different types of knowledge—to meet those differing cognitive needs of workers.

Chapter Six, "Making Knowledge Visible," discusses what the difference is between explicit and tacit knowledge. It also describes why there is a difference between explicit and tacit knowledge and how to make knowledge visible in your organization.

Chapter Seven, "Differentiating Knowledge," discusses when there are benefits to categorizing knowledge into different types. Then it describes why the four types of knowledge are different and how to identify these four in your organization.

Chapter Eight, "Differentiating Knowledge Assets," begins by discussing when providing different types of knowledge assets produces benefits. It describes why knowledge assets provide access to the four types of knowledge and how to develop the knowledge assets that provide this access.

Chapter Nine, "Differentiating Learners," discusses when learners have differing cognitive needs. It also describes why learners have differing cognitive needs and how to meet those needs for learners in your organization.

Part Three: Enabling an iLearning Organization

Part Three (Chapters Ten through Fourteen) addresses the organizational interventions necessary for an organization to become an iLearning organization. It describes how to identify expertise in an organization and create the incentives to tap that expertise. Part Three also describes how to add to a performance assessment in order to measure an individual's contribution to the knowledge of his or her team and organization.

Chapter Ten, "Locating and Marshaling Expertise," discusses when and why social network analysis is useful for locating and marshaling expertise in organizations. It also describes how to employ this analysis in your organization.

Chapter Eleven, "Ensuring Incentives to Share," discusses when the economic concept of the *market* explains the dynamics of knowledge sharing in organizations. It then describes why this concept explains the dynamics of knowledge sharing in organizations and how to provide incentives for people in your organization to share their knowledge.

Chapter Twelve, "Measuring Individual Learning and Performance," discusses when and why the knowledge that individuals contribute is the measure of their value to their organization. This chapter also describes how to go about measuring the knowledge that individuals contribute in your organization.

Chapter Thirteen, "Improving Team Learning and Performance," discusses when team learning is more than the sum of individual learning. It also describes why team learning is more than the sum of individual learning and how to use this knowledge to improve team learning in your organization.

Chapter Fourteen, "Managing Organizational Learning and Performance," discusses when organizational learning is more than the sum of team learning. It tells why this is so and describes how to improve organizational learning in your organization.

Part Four: Applying Methodologies and Deploying Technologies

Part Four (Chapters Fifteen through Nineteen) addresses the methodologies and technologies needed to support iLearning in an organization. It describes the methods used to model the work and learning processes. These methods define the format of knowledge assets, how they will be created, stored, displayed, and updated. Part Four also describes the technologies deployed to support these methods in managing the knowledge assets throughout their life cycles.

Chapter Fifteen, "Reusing Knowledge Assets," discusses when and why to employ reusable learning objects for developing knowledge assets. The chapter concludes by describing how to employ performance objectives in order to reuse knowledge assets as learning objects in your organization.

Chapter Sixteen, "Repurposing Knowledge Assets," discusses when to employ repurposed knowledge assets instead of reusable knowledge assets. It describes why repurposed knowledge assets are different from reusable knowledge assets. It also describes how to employ performance objectives in order to identify and repurpose knowledge assets in your organization.

Chapter Seventeen, "Organizing Knowledge Assets," discusses when to organize knowledge assets in organizations. It then describes why to organize knowledge assets and how to do it in your organization.

Chapter Eighteen, "Managing Knowledge Assets," discusses when to systematically update reused and repurposed knowledge assets. It also describes why to systematically update reused and repurposed knowledge assets and how to take a systematic approach in your organization.

Chapter Nineteen, "Deploying Information Technologies," discusses when to deploy technologies for managing collaboration, knowledge products, knowledge assets, role-based access, and learning and performance assessment in order to support an iLearning organization. It describes why organizations deploy technologies to support their iLearning and tells how to do it in your organization.

PART FIVE: FUTURE DIRECTIONS FOR iLEARNING

Part Five (Chapters Twenty and Twenty-One) discusses how emerging technologies and upcoming changes in the world are reinforcing and accelerating the applications of iLearning. New cell phones, media forms such as video, and 3-D virtual environments will make it easier for workers to collaboratively access knowledge assets, learn from those assets, and share what they have learned. It also describes why iLearning will have profound implications for

K–12 education, institutions of higher education, and organizations in the global economy.

Chapter Twenty, "Emerging Information Technologies," discusses where emerging technologies may support iLearning in organizations. This chapter also describes why emerging technologies may further support iLearning—and how to use them to support iLearning in your organization.

Chapter Twenty-One, "Changing Our World," discusses where iLearning is changing the world as we know it. This final chapter then describes why iLearning is changing K–12 schooling, university curriculums, and the global economy, and it talks about how to anticipate and benefit from these changes that are under way.

HOW SHOULD THIS BOOK BE READ?

Did you notice the iLearning Pyramid icon at the beginning of this introduction? It's a reminder that this book is organized around the foundations, processes, methodologies, and technologies that make up an iLearning organization. The iLearning Pyramid is also a reminder that all these things are necessary to create an iLearning organization and that they build on each other, layer upon layer. On the bottom is the foundations layer. It contains the learning theories and the categorization of different types of knowledge for different types of learners. The next layer is the processes layer. Built on the foundations layer, it describes the work processes and the learning processes. These work and learning processes reside in the same layer because they are interdependent, occur at the same time, and, in effect, live in the same organizational space. Methodologies are the next layer, built on the processes layer. Methodologies are used to model the knowledge that is used in the work and learning processes. The top and final layer is the technologies layer, built on the methodologies layer. It supports the methodologies layer through the deployment of computer technology that is used for modeling knowledge.

The five parts of this book align with the iLearning Pyramid. Although all readers will want to read the entire book, human resource professionals may want to focus on Part Three, "Enabling an iLearning Organization," and Part Five, "Future Directions for iLearning." Training professionals may want to focus on Part One, "Facilitating Collaborative Work," Part Two, "Facilitating Innovative Learning," and Part Four, "Applying Methodologies and Deploying Technologies." Information technology specialists may also want to focus on Part Four. Managers of knowledge workers may want to focus on Parts One, Two, and Three and also Five.

Except for the Introduction and Chapter One, each chapter of iLearning has the same format. First-time readers will want to look over the Learning Objectives at the beginning of the chapter. Next, they will read the Expert Advice section, which gives some insight into when and where the concepts of the chapter can be applied. They will then move on to the Concept section, which presents the theories, models, principles, and generalizations that relate to the problem at hand, and after that the Application section, which presents a solution to the problem. After reading the book, experienced managers and designers can simply look up an example or other resource that will help them address an issue in a current project. *iLearning* is written so that the reader can easily find what he or she needs to address his or her current issues at his or her level of experience.

Finally, the Expert Advice section in each chapter of *iLearning* contains questions and answers from an episode of my radio show, *The Knowledge Worker*, which is produced at KANW, 89.1 FM, in Albuquerque, New Mexico. The listeners' questions and my answers emphasize just how universal many of the performance problems that organizations experience are. They also reveal how using an iLearning paradigm can address those problems.

THE AUTHOR

Mark Salisbury has over twenty years of experience in designing and developing human performance solutions. He has published many articles in engineering, business, and education journals, such as *Computer, Journal of Knowledge Management,* and *Performance Improvement Quarterly,* and has given presentations at many international conferences, sponsored by organizations such as the American Society for Training and Development, International Society for Performance Improvement, Society for Applied Learning Technology, and Association for the Advancement of Computing in Education. He holds an MS degree in computer and information science, a PhD degree in curriculum and instruction from the University of Oregon, and also an MA in teaching economics from Western Oregon University. After completing his graduate studies, he worked for eleven years at the Boeing Company on developing software to improve human performance. His time at Boeing was split between research and development efforts and commercial products. After leaving Boeing, Mark founded Vitel, Inc., a knowledge management solutions provider that developed knowledge management systems for the U.S. Department of Defense, U.S. Department of Energy, the national laboratories, and public utility companies. In 2004, Vitel was one of two companies nominated by Los Alamos National Laboratory for the 2004 Regional Small Business Subcontractor of the Year award, and the Small Business Administration noted that "this nomination establishes Vitel as one of the nation's top small business subcontractors." Currently, Mark is associate professor in the Organizational Learning and Instructional Technology program at the University of New Mexico, where he teaches graduate courses and conducts research in the area of knowledge management.

PART ONE

FACILITATING COLLABORATIVE WORK

CHAPTER ONE

WHY iLEARNING?

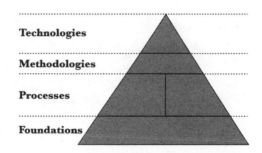

LEARNING OBJECTIVES

After reading this chapter you will be able to do the following:

- *Discuss why* iLearning is needed for the next level of innovation.
- *Discuss what* instructional systems design shares with iLearning.
- *Discuss how* to gain a systemic viewpoint on organizational performance problems.

EXPERT ADVICE

After reading this section you will be able to discuss why iLearning is needed for the next level of innovation.

Dear Mark,

I'm sold on the positive effects of knowledge management techniques— how they can save time and money for an organization. However, putting in a big effort to save later is usually not done by businesses that live and die on a quarterly financial statement. Is there a more compelling reason to better manage our knowledge other than it makes us more efficient in the long run?

Signed, "So What's the Big Idea?"

Dear "So What's the Big Idea?"

As human beings we admire the creations of individuals—Shakespeare, Michelangelo, and many others throughout history. However, some of our greatest accomplishments, especially engineering achievements, are the result of collective work—the focused brainpower of a group of humans. These collaborative achievements include the building of the Titanic, the manufacture of automobiles, and the development of the space shuttle. In engineering achievements at this level, no one person has all the knowledge to complete all aspects of the work.

However, we are hitting a wall in terms of the complexity of the work that we can intellectually share. This is evidenced in failures such as the sinking of the Titanic, automobile recalls, and technical failures with the space shuttle. To go beyond this wall, we need to model and manage the knowledge that we collectively create and share. Only then will we be able to go to the next level and solve problems such as curing cancer and deep space travel.

Remember, this wall also has implications for today's businesses here on earth that supply products and services to the marketplace. For them, it means that to offer more complex products and services, they too will have to model and manage the knowledge that their employees collectively create and share.[1]

iLearning: An Example

What is it that managers want for their organizations? Of course they want results. But how do you go about getting those results? You have everyone working and learning together in a seamless fashion. No "cowboys" working their own agendas. No reinventing the wheel. No enduring long periods of indecision while people get "up to speed." No reworking. And most important, your organization has the ability to think "larger" than one person—it has gotten beyond the Einstein model, being as smart as its smartest individual. That is, your organization has collaborative intelligence—without having *groupthink*. And because it has this intelligence, it is able to take on complex tasks that are larger than anything a single person can wrap his or her mind around. This is the essence of collaborative work.

In addition, people must be able to learn as they work if they are to foster innovation. Innovative learning begins with all team members having access to the same knowledge for the current *best way* of solving a problem. Organizations provide access to this knowledge through documents, instruction, examples, and expert advice—making the current best way of solving a problem known to all members of the team. Knowing what they know, the team members are now prepared to look at innovative ways to solve the current problem. This is where the best thinking of the past meets the best thinking of the present to create the best solutions for tomorrow. This is the essence of innovative learning—the learning that is needed to bring the next generation of complex products and services to the planet.

How would such an organization work? Consider the McBoe Company. It's a mythical outfit, the premier manufacturer of paper airplanes for the home enthusiast, but it experiences the same achievements and problems that real-life companies do. I will use McBoe throughout this book to show how the principles outlined in the Concept section of each of the following chapters can be applied in an organization.

Figure 1.1 outlines the story of how an iLearning organization might do some work. Let's begin with a McBoe engineer, a quality specialist, who needs to make a *quality plan* for a new paper airplane. The engineer goes to the company intranet site (perhaps from a cell phone) and accesses the McBoe manufacturing support system. Next the engineer clicks on the area of *Design*, then clicks on the area of *Detailed [Design]*, and then drills down to the area of *Quality Plan*. There the engineer finds all the materials that he or she will need to develop a quality plan. There is a document

FIGURE 1.1. JUST-IN-TIME DEVELOPMENT OF A QUALITY PLAN.

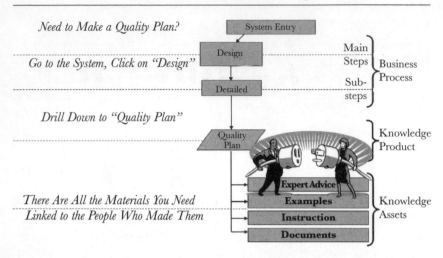

describing the performance objectives that need to be addressed in the quality plan—and how to go about addressing them. There is some instruction about the general principles behind a quality plan. The instruction also addresses the *why* issue—that is, why the project needs a quality plan. There are also some examples of successful quality plans, illustrating how others have applied the general principles of developing a quality plan to a specific project. Finally, there is some expert advice that provides direction on when and where to use one approach over another when developing a quality plan.

And that's not all the McBoe engineer finds at the Quality Plan area in the support system. He or she also finds links to the people responsible for the content—the authors of the documents, instruction, examples, and expert advice. The engineer can contact these authors directly to learn about the subtleties of the content and its application to specific projects.

In short, with these assets—the materials and the opportunity for an exchange with the people who authored them—the engineer can learn what is needed to get the job done. With adequate materials and the help of others, the engineer learns only what is needed, at the time it is needed (*just in time*) to create the quality plan for a new paper airplane.

FIGURE 1.2. EXAMPLE OF ILEARNING.

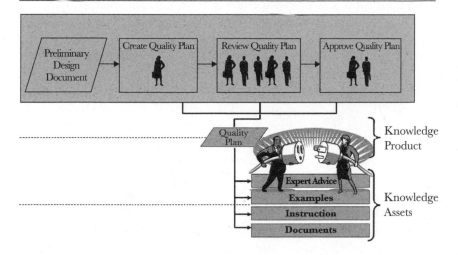

And as Figure 1.2 shows, creating a quality plan is just the first step toward completing that plan in a collaborative work environment. The next step is a review step, and finally there is an approval step. Note also that all the assets available to the engineer to create the quality plan—the materials and the opportunity for an exchange with the people who created them—are available to the other people involved in the review and approval steps. They, along with the engineer who created the quality plan, are engaging in the act of iLearning as they work together in a collaborative work environment. This collaborative team has access to the best way to create a quality plan that the company knows. If a new way is needed to create a quality plan, this team can build on the existing knowledge, in a just-in-time process, to create a plan that is truly innovative.

That's a great ending for this introductory story. If your organization is already at this high level of iLearning, do yourself a favor and skip the rest of this book. Celebrate your accomplishment and reward yourself by reading an exciting novel instead! However, if your organization is not at this high level of iLearning, then continue to read about how you can get your organization to work like the McBoe Company. But be forewarned. This is not a flavor-of-the-month or a quick-fix book. It is for those who are willing to work to gain real improvements in individual, team, and organizational learning—and the performance it brings.

This example of the McBoe Company's experience illustrates what we all want to achieve in our organizations. However, what we have seen so far is simply the technology that serves up the information and connects the people. Technology-based solutions leave us wondering how the information gets into the system—and more important, how it is updated and maintained. It's quickly apparent that the technology is simply the tip of the iceberg, a particularly visible but small part of the much larger iLearning organization. Moreover, technology is not the essence of iLearning but a facilitator of it; technology is a means of connecting workers and providing information. As Figure 1.3 shows, this book supplies readers with the actual foundations, processes, and methodologies that construct the iLearning work and learning environment, as well as the information about the technologies (learning management system [LMS], content manager, and collaboration software) needed to support that environment. Furthermore, this book describes (in Part Three) how to conduct the organizational interventions that enable an iLearning organization.

FIGURE 1.3. LAYERS OF THE iLEARNING PYRAMID.

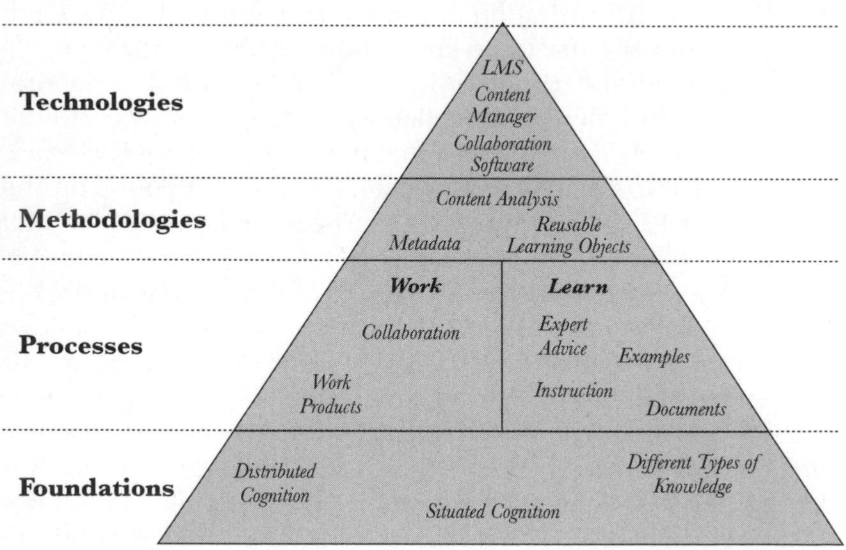

Technologies
LMS
Content Manager
Collaboration Software

Methodologies
Content Analysis
Metadata
Reusable Learning Objects

Processes
Work
Collaboration
Work Products

Learn
Expert Advice
Examples
Instruction
Documents

Foundations
Distributed Cognition
Different Types of Knowledge
Situated Cognition

Building on the Familiar

Like all good approaches for solving a complex problem, this book builds on a methodology that has provided proven results for previous problem solving. That methodology is *instructional systems design* (ISD), and it has been successfully used to solve training and performance problems for decades in organizations. (See my article for a detailed and referenced discussion of moving from ISD interventions to managing the knowledge in organizations.[2])

The major phases of ISD are typically identified as analysis, design, development, implementation, and evaluation. The design phase uses the information from the analysis phase to formulate a plan for presenting instruction to learners. Instruction involves organizing and providing sets of information and activities that guide, support, and augment students' internal mental processes. Learning has occurred when students have incorporated new information that enables them to master new knowledge and skills. This view of learning as a change in internal mental processes that results in improved performance is a cornerstone for modern applications of ISD intended to solve organizational performance problems.

Managers using an ISD approach to solve a performance problem in an organization begin by noting the difference between the current state of performance and the desired state of performance. For example, an organization might determine that the current state of human performance in creating quality plans is far below the desired state for the organization (see Figure 1.4). In other words, the organization has found that its quality plans are not very useful for doing what they are supposed to do—ensuring high-quality production. There is a big gap between how good the quality plans are currently and how good they need to be to guide meaningful testing of products before they are delivered to customers.

As Figure 1.4 shows, a quality plan is a *knowledge product,* or *artifact.* That is, it embodies conclusions, judgments, and decisions about what goes into a particular quality plan for a specific product. Also, every quality plan has a set of criteria, or *performance objectives,* that need to be met by the plan's human developers for its successful completion. These performance objectives are sometimes implicit,

FIGURE 1.4. IDENTIFYING INSTRUCTIONAL CONTENT.

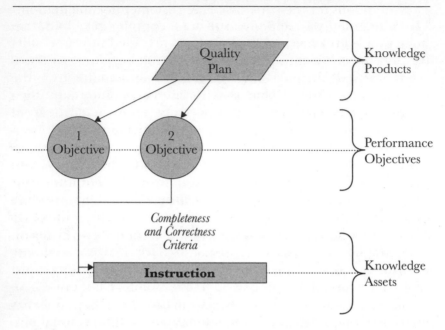

that is, in the eye of the beholder. Even when they cannot easily articulate performance objectives, people indicate that they recognize the existence of such objectives when they use such phrases as, "I know a good quality plan when I see one," or, "Shouldn't a quality plan have a . . . ?" Performance objectives spell out what needs to be done and how well it should be done for a good quality plan.

One way to go about identifying performance objectives for a quality plan is to conduct a *content analysis.* This analysis starts off with the question, What knowledge does a person need to know to create a quality plan? The answer involves, first, the identification of the main broad areas of knowledge needed. One of these areas needs to contain the criteria for measuring product performance, called *completeness* and *correctness* criteria. Once the main areas are identified, they are broken down by topic. For the completeness and correctness criteria, topics include *product documentation, product performance,* and *product life expectancy.* Next, each topic is rewritten as a performance objective. In the McBoe Company example the topic *product documentation* might be rewritten as this performance objective: "State the level of performance, criterion, and conditions for the paper airplane customer documentation." (For a complete description of the steps for conducting a content analysis, see Rothwell and Kazanas.[3])

Figure 1.4 illustrates that in this example two product documentation performance objectives have been identified from the completeness and correctness criteria identified for creating a quality plan. Performance objectives make a precise statement of what a learner should *do* in order to accomplish the stated performance. Each one contains a *performance component*, a *criterion component*, and a *condition component*. The performance component describes how proficiency will be demonstrated. Continuing our McBoe example, this component is the entire statement of the objective: "State the level of performance, criterion, and conditions for the airplane customer documentation." The criterion component in this example is implied by the word *state*—meaning that the "level of performance, criterion, and conditions" must be clearly defined to ensure a good quality plan. The condition component describes what conditions must exist when proficiency is demonstrated. This example has implied conditions in that no special conditions are needed in the quality specialist's environment for stating the performance, criterion, and conditions for airplane customer documentation. An explicit condition that could be required for this objective is "written with access to a simplified English dictionary." That is, the performance expected of the quality specialist would be required only if the he or she had access to a simplified English dictionary. Here is the product documentation performance objective ultimately created, reviewed, and approved by the quality plan team:

> A purchased paper airplane can be assembled, with instructions in American English or Spanish, with no mistakes in 15 minutes by an individual with a fourth-grade reading level.

Figure 1.4 also illustrates that in an ISD approach, instruction is developed for learners to achieve the identified performance objectives. As discussed earlier, instruction is one of many knowledge assets that can be used by learners to achieve performance objectives.

Finally, be aware that an organizational intervention delivered by ISD is typically a piecemeal approach to managing the knowledge of an organization. ISD begins by discovering a problem in an organization, then locating the work that needs to be improved, determining the knowledge needed to do the work, and finally designing instruction to teach that knowledge—all to solve a specific problem. Although ISD is good for solving the latest crisis discovered, it typically doesn't prevent the next crisis.

For instance, in the quality plan example of Figure 1.1, once workers are trained in making better quality plans, then the organization will have the benefit of better quality plans. However, making better quality plans will not prevent another performance gap from rearing its ugly head in another part of the organization. For example, suppose that after the various quality plans were improved, no overall improvement in product quality occurred. After some floundering it was discovered that there was another performance gap, this time in developing the *testing reports*. Only after the ISD process of analysis is invoked again will it be discovered that this new gap is similar to the gap discovered earlier in the knowledge of workers completing the quality plan. Once this similarity is noted, then a determination can be made of how much instruction, if any, can be used for both quality plans and testing reports. At that time, performance objectives similar to the ones previously written for workers completing quality plans can be written for workers completing testing reports. However, it is not until the lack of improvement is found that it becomes apparent that the two performance problems are related, that lack of knowledge for creating quality plans is related to lack of knowledge for developing testing reports. Creating instruction for the quality plans but not the testing reports did not lead to improved organizational performance.

This latter example shows that even though ISD is effective for solving acute and specific organizational problems with instructional applications, it is not very effective for identifying the systemic relationships between organizational performance problems. It is this lack of a systems view that keeps instructional designers on a never-ending treadmill of responding to one performance crisis after another. They are able to keep the enterprise afloat but don't have the time, the energy, and most important, the big-picture perspective to make the necessary systemic improvements for improving organizational performance. What is needed is a systemic viewpoint from which to analyze, design, and implement improvements for organizational performance problems.

THE LIFE CYCLE OF KNOWLEDGE

Figure 1.5 shows the life cycle of knowledge in organizations. It is the starting point for building this systemic viewpoint from which to analyze, design, and implement improvements for organizational performance problems. The first phase is the creation of new knowledge. This takes place when an organization's members solve a new, unique problem, which may be either a single problem or a problem that is a small part of a larger problem, such as a problem generated by an ongoing project. The second phase is the preservation of this newly created knowledge. This phase feeds the third phase, the dissemination and application of this new knowledge. Dissemination and application involves sharing this new knowledge with the other members of the organization. It also involves sharing the solutions with the stakeholders affected by the problems that were solved. Disseminated knowledge then becomes an input for solving new problems in the next knowledge creation phase. An organization's ability to solve problems increases with the use of this disseminated knowledge. In this way, each knowledge life cycle phase provides input for the next phrase—creating an ongoing cycle. Because this cycle continues to build upon itself, it becomes a knowledge spiral in

FIGURE 1.5. LIFE CYCLE OF KNOWLEDGE IN ORGANIZATIONS.

Knowledge
Preservation

Knowledge
Creation

Knowledge
Dissemination

the organization, as described by Nonaka and Takeuchi in their 1995 book, *The Knowledge-Creating Company*.[4] However, for organizations to build on what they know, they must know how their knowledge is organized, how to learn from that knowledge, and how to add this learning to what they already know. This book, *iLearning*, is written to be a road map with which organizations can achieve this paradigm of innovative learning.[5]

Notes

1. Each "expert advice" section is derived from my radio show, *The Knowledge Worker*, produced at the KANW public radio station in Albuquerque, New Mexico. Names and details have been changed to improve the value of these radio segments as examples.
2. M. Salisbury, "From Instructional Systems Design to Managing the Life Cycle of Knowledge in Organizations," *Performance Improvement Quarterly, 13*(3), February 2008, 202–219.
3. W. Rothwell and H. Kanzanas, *Mastering the Instructional Design Process* (San Francisco: Pfeiffer, 2004).
4. I. Nonaka and H. Takeuchi, *The Knowledge-Creating Company* (New York: Oxford University Press, 1995).
5. A quick and referenced discussion of the concepts presented in this book can be found in my article, M. Salisbury, "Creating an Innovative Learning Organization," *International Journal on E-Learning, 8*(4), Sept. 2009 (forthcoming).

CHAPTER TWO

BECOMING ONE MIND

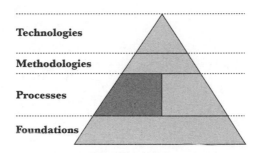

LEARNING OBJECTIVES

After reading this chapter you will be able to do the following:

- *Discuss where* the theory of distributed cognition is a good foundation for facilitating collaborative work.
- *Describe why* the theory of distributed cognition is a good foundation for facilitating collaborative work.
- *Describe how* to apply the theory of distributed cognition to facilitate collaborative work in your organization.

EXPERT ADVICE

After reading this section you will be able to discuss where the theory of distributed cognition is a good foundation for facilitating collaborative work.

Dear Mark,

In a talk that you recently gave, I heard you say that the foundation of collaboration lies in creating a "mind of one." Sounds kind of Zen to me. What did you mean by that?

Signed, "Waiting for Wisdom"

Dear "Waiting for Wisdom,"

I admit that my answer did sound kind of Zen-like. However, good design is built on sound theoretical principles. I like to apply Edwin Hutchins's theory of distributed cognition to the design of collaborative work systems. Hutchins—a professor at the University of California, San Diego—studied how a crew collaborated to operate a large ship at sea.[1]

According to Hutchins's theory, cognition is distributed across individuals. That is, no one individual has complete knowledge about how to accomplish a complex task such as operating a large ship. Hutchins also finds that cognition is distributed across the artifacts of people's work. On the ship that means the instruments provide critical decision-making information to the crew members. And according to Hutchins, cognition is in the history of those artifacts. On the ship the previous value of an instrument gives a context for the present value of that instrument.

Remember to make sure these foundations are in place to ensure successful collaboration for your team. Get agreement on your work process. Capture important decision-making information in your artifacts. In an office environment these artifacts are your working documents. And finally, capture the history of your artifacts—that may mean having a system for storage and retrieval of older versions of your documents. Do these things, and you will work with the mind of one.

CONCEPT

After reading this section you will be able to describe why the theory of distributed cognition is a good foundation for facilitating collaborative work. While you are reading this section you will learn about the following aspects of distributed cognition:

- Cognition is distributed across individuals.
- Cognition is distributed in artifacts.
- Cognition is captured in the history of artifacts.

Cognition Is Distributed Across Individuals

Figure 2.1 shows the business process, with the two main steps of *design* and *build* for a manufacturing process. The design step contains two substeps—*preliminary* and *detailed.* The build step also contains two substeps—*implementation* and *delivery.* According to the theory of distributed cognition, the subtleties of a complex process do not all reside in the head of one individual. (See, for example, Salomon's collection of essays on distributed cognition by a variety of authors.[2]) Rather, the process is known in its entirety only by the organization that works the process. Each member of the organization knows only how to do his or her part of the process. As a result, the larger process is known only collectively, and the ability to make informed decisions within the process is distributed across all people who work the process.

Cognition Is Distributed in Artifacts

Figure 2.2 illustrates the second aspect of the theory of distributed cognition: cognition is also distributed in the artifacts of the workflow process. Artifacts (which may also be called *knowledge products*) are used to capture decisions and information about the work that has been done in the workflow process. For example, the *design document*, the *quality plan*, the *testing report*, and the *user document*

FIGURE 2.1.   COGNITION IS DISTRIBUTED ACROSS INDIVIDUALS.

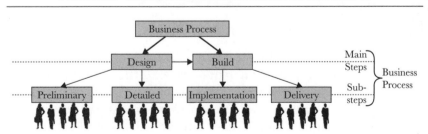

FIGURE 2.2. COGNITION IS DISTRIBUTED IN ARTIFACTS.

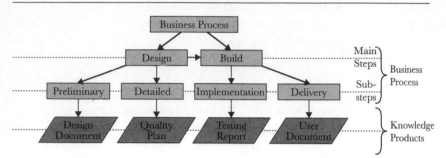

FIGURE 2.3. COGNITION IS CAPTURED IN THE HISTORY OF ARTIFACTS.

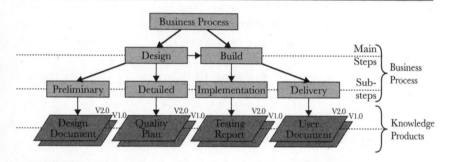

are artifacts that capture workflow decisions and information. As Figure 2.2 shows, artifacts are distributed across the organization's workflow process. Because each artifact contains embedded information about decisions that concern a unique aspect of the process, each one also represents a subset of the cognition needed to complete the entire workflow process.

Cognition Is Captured in the History of Artifacts

Figure 2.3 shows the third aspect of the theory of distributed cognition—the history of an artifact reveals the context for decisions and information about the process over time. As shown in Figure 2.3, for example, the quality plan is currently in version 2.0. This means the quality plan team has made some major changes since version 1.0 of the quality plan was created. Obviously, some

of the version 1.0 decisions and process information were different from those of version 2.0. The history of the changes in an
artifact tells the reasons that those changes were made. Frequently,
it turns out that artifacts are historically related to one another.
That means that a change in one artifact, say a design document,
will affect another artifact—in the Figure 2.3 example, it will affect
the quality plan. In this way the histories of artifacts provide important rationales for the present forms of those artifacts.

APPLICATION

After reading this section you will be able to describe how to apply
the theory of distributed cognition to facilitate collaborative work
in your organization. While you are reading this section you will
learn the following techniques:

- How to distribute cognition across individuals
- How to distribute cognition in artifacts
- How to capture cognition in the history of artifacts

HOW TO DISTRIBUTE COGNITION ACROSS INDIVIDUALS

Figure 2.1 also shows the business process, with the two main steps
of design and build, for the paper airplane manufacturing process
at the McBoe Company. According to the theory of distributed
cognition the goal is to have cognition evenly distributed across
the individuals who complete the workflow process. That means
all the workers should know how to do the work in their part of
the process, but they are not expected to know how to do someone else's work. At the McBoe Company, the people who carry out
the substep in which the design is *detailed* do a great job of designing a new paper airplane but have little knowledge about how
to deliver their new airplane to their customers. Conversely, the
people in the substep of *delivery* know how to get a paper airplane
to the marketplace but do not know how to design a new paper
airplane. In short, as members of a manufacturing organization,
each one knows how to do his or her part in the larger process,
and collectively they know how to both design and deliver a new
paper airplane to the marketplace.

A couple of years ago at McBoe, new employees were hired to do the detailed substep of design, and they were not familiar with the process for creating a detailed design. At the same time, new employees were being hired for the delivery substep, and they were not familiar with that process. While new hires are not uncommon at McBoe, having two new groups come in together created a problem. Work was completed late and more mistakes were found. It was easy to see that cognition of the larger process was not evenly distributed across all the individuals in the manufacturing process. Said another way, there were large pockets of missing knowledge about the manufacturing process because some individuals didn't know how to do their own jobs. McBoe solved this problem by training the new hires about how to complete their own work within the process.

McBoe found that to have cognition evenly distributed across its manufacturing process, each worker must have the knowledge to do his or her own work within that process. When there are pockets of missing knowledge, an intervention needs to be prepared and conducted to supply individuals with the knowledge to do their own jobs.

Relate to Your Organization. How about your organization—is cognition evenly distributed across its business process? Or are there pockets of missing knowledge? If there are pockets, is training an option for those individuals who lack knowledge to gain the knowledge to do their own jobs?

How to Distribute Cognition in Artifacts

Looking back at Figure 2.2, we can see how cognition is also distributed in the artifacts of the workflow process for the McBoe paper airplane manufacturing company. At McBoe, each artifact captures decisions and process information. For example, the artifact that captures the results of the work in the *preliminary design* substep is the design document. This *embedded knowledge* about design is used by the engineers who develop the quality plan in the following detailed design substep. Looking across all the artifacts of the process—the design document, the quality plan, the testing report, and the user document—we see that they are distributed across the manufacturing process. Imagine the McBoe employees trying to complete their manufacturing process without these artifacts! It's apparent that there is a large amount of cognition in these artifacts distributed across the McBoe manufacturing process.

The artifacts of McBoe's manufacturing process were not always the same as the ones highlighted in Figure 2.2. Just last year the McBoe process treated the quality plan as part of the design document. However, McBoe management felt the organization was losing some of its commitment to quality during the development of the design document. Said another way, it was not adequately capturing decisions about quality in its existing artifacts. In response to this problem, the McBoe management decided to break out the work on quality, put it in a separate process, and capture the reasoning about quality in a new artifact, which became known as the quality plan.

In other words, McBoe found that it was short an artifact—the quality plan. Without it, cognition was not evenly distributed in the artifacts across the manufacturing process. McBoe had, in effect, a hole in its process where reasoning leaked out. The addition of a new artifact, the quality plan, plugged that hole and made the newly captured reasoning part of the McBoe process.

Relate to Your Organization. As McBoe did in adding a new artifact to its process, your organization must examine its workflow process and ask the following questions. Do we have the best number of artifacts for our process? Are they the right artifacts? And are those artifacts distributed evenly across our process? Are there any holes in our process that allow reasoning to leak out and that need to be plugged up?

How to Capture Cognition in the History of Artifacts

Figure 2.3 shows the third aspect of the theory of distributed cognition in the paper airplane manufacturing process for the McBoe Company, where cognition is captured in the history of the artifacts in the manufacturing process. Note that in Figure 2.3, the quality plan is currently in version 2.0. As discussed earlier, that means some major changes have been made since version 1.0, and the history of such changes in an artifact tells why those changes were made. In many instances the reason for a change, or *update*, is that a related artifact has changed. At McBoe the design document was updated from version 1.0 to 2.0 to reflect paper airplane design changes due to changes in customer preferences. Because the quality plan is based in part on that design, it also required modification and was updated from version 1.0 to version 2.0. At McBoe the history of an artifact is one way to reveal the reasoning behind the artifact's present form.

Keeping track of the history of its artifacts allows the McBoe Company to uncover dependencies between artifacts in the business process. McBoe learned that the quality plan is dependent on the design document. That captured reasoning allows McBoe to answer questions such as this one: What are the effects, in terms of time and quality, of design changes on the manufacturing process?

Relate to Your Organization. Does your organization have mechanisms in place to capture the history of its artifacts? Does it have ways in place to uncover the dependencies between the artifacts of its process? Can it answer questions such as this: What are the effects, in terms of time and quality, of design changes on our process?

Notes
1. E. Hutchins, *Cognition in the Wild* (Cambridge, Mass.: MIT Press, 1996).
2. G. Salomon, *Distributed Cognitions* (New York: Cambridge University Press, 1996).

CHAPTER THREE

AGREEING ON THE WORKFLOW PROCESS

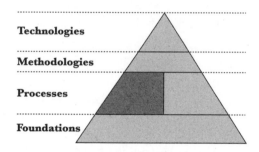

LEARNING OBJECTIVES

After reading this chapter you will be able to do the following:

- *Discuss when* a nontraditional way of defining an organization's process might work better than a traditional approach.
- *Describe why* it's difficult to agree on a workflow process in an organization.
- *Describe how* to agree on a workflow process in your organization.

EXPERT ADVICE

After reading this section you will be able to discuss when a non-traditional way of defining an organization's process might work better than a traditional approach.

Dear Mark,

It seems to me that the "trick" to working together smarter is to simply agree on your process and put in some technology to manage the work around the process. However, getting people to agree on the process IS the hard part. Any suggestions for how to get this done?

Signed, "How Do We Agree to Agree?"

Dear "How Do We Agree to Agree?"

Sometimes, a traditional approach will work just fine with some teams. Typically, a traditional approach will have the following steps: (1) Get your team together. (2) Open the discussion on defining the team's process. (3) Work toward narrowing the options that are considered. And (4) bring it in for a landing by closing with an agreement on the process.

However, another way to do this is to take a story-based approach. I've used this with a team that "resisted" traditional approaches to defining its process. The approach goes like this. Have one of your "resisters" tell a brief story about working his or her process. For example, the resister may tell a story in which "Paul" submitted a request, and "Debbie" evaluated the request and then forwarded it to "John" to work out a solution. John created a solution and forwarded it to "Fred," who reviewed it and sent it on to "Elaine," who approved it. Take this story as a starting point and have the others add to it.

Remember also to get those stories where things didn't work as they should. For example, perhaps before Elaine approved the solution, she modified it and put it in the system without telling anyone—thereby circumventing the process. Just like stories of failure in our personal lives, organizational stories of failure point us to the path of redemption.

CONCEPT

After reading this section you will be able to describe why it's difficult to agree on a workflow process in an organization. While you are reading this section you will learn about the following considerations for defining a process in an organization:

- Traditional ways fail to define processes.
- Storytelling can define processes.

TRADITIONAL WAYS FAIL TO DEFINE PROCESSES

Figure 3.1 shows a process that an organization has defined for creating a quality plan. The process begins with the *preliminary design document* as input for the *create criteria* step. *Review criteria* is the next step. And *approve quality plan* is the last step. The process shown in Figure 3.1 is a linear, formal process for creating a quality plan, but a less formal and more parallel process could also be used. For example, workers could participate in all the steps at once, and creating criteria, reviewing the criteria, and approving those criteria could all go on at the same time until the dust settles. Or workers could use a mixed approach with linear, formal steps but less formality and more parallelism within each step. For example, in the first step one person might submit a document for review, in the second step a group of reviewers might work in parallel submitting comments within a defined time period, and in the third step a single person might have the authority to approve the document. The important point here is to define the objectives of the collaborative process (for example, to get as much review from as many perspectives in as little time as possible

FIGURE 3.1.   DEFINING THE BUSINESS PROCESS.

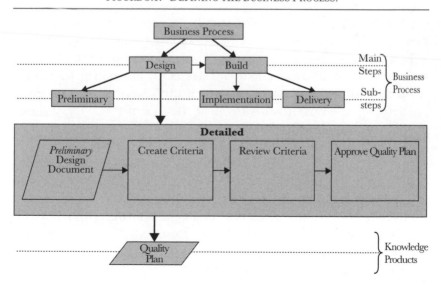

or to have each department approve the document) and then to define a process that will accomplish those objectives.

In many cases a traditional facilitation approach will work just fine to define such a process. Typically, this approach begins with some kind of brainstorming exercise. Next, some means of narrowing the field of possibilities is carried out. And finally, this approach ends with some agreements as to what the process will be for the organization. (Many good books have been written on facilitation. Just type "facilitation" in the search box for any online bookstore, and you will receive a substantial number of hits.)

STORYTELLING CAN DEFINE PROCESSES

Sometimes a traditional approach just doesn't work. Oh, everyone agrees that defining a process is a task with a lot of merit—it's just that either no one ever has the time to do it or the task seems so big and laborious that a group just can't seem to get started on it. In this slow-start situation, a nontraditional approach such as storytelling may get people started on agreeing on a process. The way to begin is to ask someone to tell a recent story about a successful result after working with others in the organization. A good "focusing" method is to ask the storyteller to make one of the work artifacts the "star" of the story. Once this initial install-ment of the story is recorded, ask others to add their parts to the story, parts that may not be known to the entire group. Remem-ber, the knowledge of how to do the larger process is distributed across the group—no one person knows all the details of the process. As the additional stories are told, others in the group should be allowed to ask questions of the storytellers. This gives participants the opportunity to clarify details of the story, thereby addressing any ambiguity about the process that a storyteller might have introduced.

Furthermore, allowing others to question the storyteller brings out into the open what is actually being done. This gives people the opportunity to compare what is actually being done to what they think should be done. This can be a very enlightening and helpful exercise. A few years ago, for example, a large manufactur-ing company conducted a program to identify the top performers of certain important processes and to see how they did it. What they found was that the top people didn't always follow the "right way" to do a process. In many cases this discrepancy provided a basis for a process improvement.[1]

Finally, in using this nontraditional technique, managers should make a big effort to get those stories where things didn't work out well. Addressing these failures will help the organization identify ambiguous places in its process. In this way, telling failure stories can be the basis for clarifying how the process should work. (To learn more about this topic, see *Storytelling in Organizations*, by Brown, Denning, Groh, and Prusak.[2])

APPLICATION

After reading this section you will be able to describe how to agree on a workflow process in your organization. While you are reading this section you will learn about applying the following techniques for agreeing on a workflow process:

- How to recognize failure to define processes
- How to use storytelling to define processes

HOW TO RECOGNIZE FAILURE TO DEFINE PROCESSES

The process shown in Figure 3.1 is very similar to what the McBoe Company ended up with when it defined a process to create a quality plan for the manufacture of a new paper airplane. The process begins with the preliminary design document as input for the create criteria step of developing a quality plan. Review criteria is the next step. And approve quality plan is the last step.

In its first attempt to define this process, McBoe tried a traditional, facilitation-based approach with its quality team. This first attempt failed. For various reasons, team members just couldn't get started on defining the process. One time, process definition was put at the end of a long agenda and never came up for discussion. Another time, it was the "victim" of a long discussion about the market for a new airplane and was pushed off to a later meeting. In the end, the team just couldn't get to it, and it kept sliding into the future.

Relate to Your Organization. Are you ready to try to gain agreement on a process in your organization? Have you tried this before? Was it successful? Or did it fail for all the reasons that plagued McBoe? If so, you may be facing a failure with using traditional ways to define your process.

How to Use Storytelling to Define Processes

What turned this situation around for McBoe was using storytelling techniques to get people started on agreeing on a process. Managers began by asking one of the quality team members, John, to tell a recent story about a successful result after working with others in the quality team. John was instructed to make one of the work artifacts the "star" of the story. As a good quality team member should, John made a quality plan the star of the story. He started at the beginning of the story and named names. It went something like this: Paul submitted a request for a quality plan, Debbie evaluated the request and passed it to John, who wrote a quality plan.

Once this story was recorded, others were asked to add their parts of the story that might not be known by the entire team. So Paul added his story, telling how he goes about submitting a request for a quality plan. Debbie told her story about how she evaluates a request. And John added his story about how he wrote a quality plan for the request. As the stories were told, others in the group were allowed to ask questions of each storyteller. For example, as Debbie was queried the team teased out the criteria she uses to evaluate a request. Allowing the quality team members to question the storytellers brought out into the open what was actually being done with quality plans. This gave the team the opportunity to compare the actual process to the process the team members thought they should be completing.

The McBoe quality team also made a big effort to get those stories where things didn't work out well. For example, in one such story Elaine told the team members that she had modified a quality plan written by John and only then had approved it. Elaine's modifications created a problem because John was never made aware of them—and he was the author of the quality plan. After listening to this story of a process failure, the quality team came to the conclusion that a successful story for this situation would have Elaine indicate, first, that the quality plan was not acceptable without certain modifications. Next, Elaine would send the plan back to John, who—if he agreed with the modifications— would incorporate them into the plan. Then John would send the quality plan back to Elaine for approval. End of story. In this way the McBoe quality team used a failure story as a basis for clarifying how the process should work given that the person in the role of approver finds an initial quality plan to be unacceptable.

Relate to Your Organization. In your organization is there someone you can call upon to tell his or her story about successfully working with others to complete an artifact? What about the others— will they join in and add their stories as well? Are there stories to be told about things not working out well? Will people tell them? And do these stories reveal some process clarifications or improvements that could be made?

Notes

1. F. Sanchez, "Capturing Expert Knowledge," *Proceedings of the Ninth International Symposium on Semiconductor Manufacturing*, IEEE, 2000, pp. 84–87.
2. B. Brown, S. Denning, K. Groh, and L. Prusak, *Storytelling in Organizations: Why Storytelling Is Transforming 21st Century Organizations and Management* (Burlington, Mass.: Elsevier Butterworth-Heinemann, 2005).

CHAPTER FOUR

DEFINING ROLES WITHIN THE PROCESS

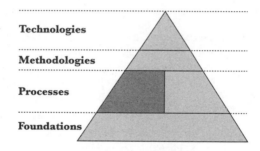

LEARNING OBJECTIVES

After reading this chapter you will be able to do the following:

- *Discuss when* defining roles within a process will improve the quality and timeliness of work.
- *Describe why* defining roles within a process will improve the quality and timeliness of work.
- *Describe how* to apply roles within a process in your organization.

EXPERT ADVICE

After reading this section you will be able to discuss when defining roles within a process will improve the quality and timeliness of work.

Dear Mark,

We have set up a collaboration area for our team to create documents. We have agreed on a workflow for creating the documents, including which documents are to be created before others. However, our problem is that some people in our team are "helping out" by updating documents that they didn't work on. I thought we had addressed this problem with a team meeting, but still people update documents after they have been declared "done." Any ideas about how we can get better control of our updates?

Signed, "Too Much Unauthorized Help"

Dear "Too Much Unauthorized Help,"

You have defined your process—good for you—but now you have to define the roles that your team members will play in that process.

I recommend that for each document that your team creates, you select the coordinator, and this coordinator then selects the authors, reviewers, and approvers. These roles can be filled by different people for each document— but the point is that they are selected ahead of time for *each* document. As I said, the coordinator should be the one who makes these selections. The authors will be the team members who will create the document—and who will be responsible for all updates to the document. The reviewers will simply review the documents and make suggestions for revision. And the approvers—although having approval authority—*will not* make revisions to the actual documents. Only the authors will make revisions. In this way, you can get control over who updates the documents and when.

Remember, sometimes the best invitations are those that are never delivered! With this in mind, your coordinator can invite only those to the party who have active and well-defined roles.

Concept

After reading this section you will be able to describe why defining roles within a process will improve the quality and timeliness of work. While reading this section you will learn about the following aspects of defining process roles:

- Identification of roles
- Rules of engagement between roles

IDENTIFICATION OF ROLES

After defining a collaboration process, the next step is to identify the roles within that process. In general, the more linear and formal a collaboration process is, the more important it is to identify the roles. If the process is informal—if, for example, everyone participates equally in all the steps at once until the dust settles—then there is little need to identify specific roles for workers. However, if there are reasons to complete specific steps before others or if certain individuals or groups have to be involved during certain steps, then the collaboration process needs to be more formal and specific roles are more necessary. As mentioned at the beginning of the previous chapter, most organizations will probably employ a mix of formal and informal collaboration processes to get all the collaborative work done.

Figure 4.1 shows a formal collaborative process requiring the use of specific roles. It begins by identifying the author(s) who will create quality criteria as the first step in creating a quality plan for the organization. Note that the selection of an author is dependent on the document to be created. Different documents will require different authors. For example, the preliminary design document will be authored by a designer, and the quality plan will be authored by a quality specialist, and so forth. The rule of thumb here is that each person given the role of document author should be an expert in the document subject matter.

As displayed in Figure 4.1, identifying the reviewer(s) for the review of the quality criteria is the second step in creating a quality plan. Note that for each document a chosen set of people fill specific roles. For one document a particular person may be the author; for another document that same person may be a reviewer. What if the same person is both author and approver? Then the job of identifying people to fill the roles for that document was

FIGURE 4.1.   DEFINING SPECIFIC ROLES WITHIN A PROCESS.

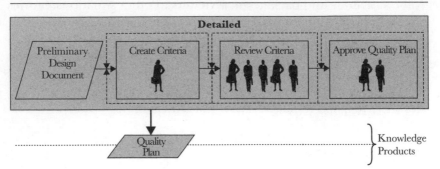

not well done. Human nature being what it is, the author-reviewer will be predisposed to like the original document better than the one with the changes suggested by the reviewers.

Identifying the approver(s) for the approval of the quality criteria is the third step in creating a quality plan (Figure 4.1). In real life the people most likely to be approving documents will not be involved in authoring or reviewing them. In many cases, the person with the authority for approving work will be at a higher level in the organization's management than the other team members are. Maybe he or she is not always the best person for the job—but that's the way it is in real life.

RULES OF ENGAGEMENT BETWEEN ROLES

The dotted lines and arrows around the roles in Figure 4.1 indicate that defining how the roles will relate to one another in the process of creating a document is the final step in role definition. This is where all the issues of process and authority come together. This is the point when what we might call the *rules of engagement* are defined, rules that cover what to do when exceptions to the process crop up. If you, as an approver, receive a reviewed document that you don't want to approve, what do you do? As discussed in Chapter Three, stories of failure uncover many such instances that haven't been previously considered. The lines and arrows in Figure 4.1 illustrate that in the process depicted (and perhaps as defined in a previous process document), a document that is not approved goes back to the original author in some situations and back to the reviewers in other situations. Stories about failure bring out many of the exceptional situations that need to be considered, and the proper course of action should not remain in the head of the storyteller but should be agreed on by the organization and recorded in something permanent, such as a process document. (For an overview of defining roles and modeling workflow, see *Workflow Management,* by van der Aalst and van Hee.[1])

Application

After reading this section you will be able to describe how to apply roles within a process in your organization. While you are reading this section you will learn the following techniques:

- How to identify specific roles
- How to define rules of engagement between roles

How to Identify Specific Roles

At the McBoe Company a formal collaborative process with specific roles was needed for creating a quality plan. As also displayed in Figure 4.1, the process began by identifying the author(s) for creating a quality plan. At McBoe, different documents require different authors. Paul and Roger are designers at McBoe, and Paul might be selected to create the preliminary design document for this quality plan and Roger might be selected to create the preliminary design document for a different quality plan, based on the judgment of their manager. However, because neither one of them knows much about creating a quality plan, one of the quality specialists at McBoe—such as Betty or Bob—would be identified as the author of this quality plan. Authors are identified by their depth of knowledge in the subject about which they are asked to write.

At the McBoe Company, identifying the reviewer(s) is the second step in defining the specific roles for creating a quality plan. Again, as with assigning document creators, if Fred and Betty are reviewers, Fred might be selected to review this quality plan, and Betty might be selected to review some other quality plan, based on the judgment of their manager. Or the manager might assign both Fred and Betty to review this quality plan. Reviewers are identified by their knowledge of the subject and also by their knowledge of related issues. Reviewers need breadth as well as depth of knowledge on the subject to be reviewed. In some situations, more than one reviewer might be needed to provide the needed breadth on a subject.

Identifying the approver(s) is the third step in defining the specific roles for creating a quality plan at McBoe. Again, as with assigning authors and reviewers, if Elaine and Margaret are approvers, Elaine may be selected to approve this quality plan and Margaret might be selected to approve another quality plan, based on the judgment of their manager. At McBoe, Elaine and Margaret were selected to approve documents because they were at a high level in management and had the authority for approving the work.

Relate to Your Organization. How about your organization—has it ended the confusion around the roles that people play in its process? Does it need to define specific roles such as authors, reviewers, and approvers of process documents? If specific roles are needed, do authors have deep knowledge of the subject? Do reviewers have breadth as well as depth of knowledge on the subject to be reviewed? Do approvers have approval authority for the work described in the documents they will see?

How to Define Rules of Engagement Between Roles

At the McBoe Company, identifying how the roles relate to one another (the dotted lines and arrows in Figure 4.1) is the last step in defining the specific roles for creating a quality plan. McBoe uncovered a problem early on in this area. Betty was named as a reviewer of a document she had authored. What do you think happened? You students of human nature already suspect the outcome. Betty became protective of her document while it was under review, trying to persuade the other reviewer, Fred, that no changes of substance were needed. When Elaine received the reviewed document, she was concerned that it contained noticeable inconsistencies and ambiguities yet showed no significant review comments. This incident led McBoe to change its rules of engagement so that authors could not be reviewers of their own documents. The rules of engagement have to be consistent with the goals of the organization.

Relate to Your Organization. Has your organization defined the rules of engagement for the roles in its process? Are these rules consistent with the goals of your organization? Do you need to pull out some stories to clarify how things should work when exceptions occur in your organization's process, such as when an author of a document is also a reviewer of that document?

Note

1. W. van der Aalst and K. van Hee, *Workflow Management: Models, Methods, and Systems* (Cambridge, Mass.: MIT Press, 2004).

CHAPTER FIVE

WORKING THE PROCESS

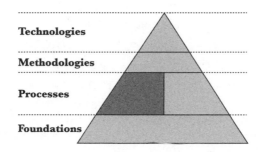

LEARNING OBJECTIVES

After reading this chapter you will be able to do the following:

- *Discuss when* measuring performance is the key for improving processes.
- *Describe why* measuring performance is the key for improving processes.
- *Describe how* to measure performance for improving processes in your organization.

EXPERT ADVICE

After reading this section you will be able to discuss when measuring performance is the key for improving processes.

Dear Mark,

I heard you once say that performance objectives are the real "work drivers" of an organization and that they are the key for knowledge management systems. Would you explain what you meant by this?

Signed, "What Are You Driving At?"

Dear "What Are You Driving At?"

Have you ever pulled out a string of yarn that was part of your sweater? If you pulled a lot of the yarn out before it broke, you will find that your wonderful sweater—the one that was given to you as a present—is now falling to pieces. That string of yarn ran the distance through your sweater.

It's the same with performance objectives—the drivers of work. If we look at the intermediate work products that get completed along the way in any business process, we will see things like design documents, testing reports, and such. Each one of these products has a set of performance objectives that have to be met in order for that product to be successfully completed. These are things that have to be done and done correctly. If one of the performance objectives is not met, then it is like the missing yarn in the sweater, and the final product has a flaw—sometimes a potentially fatal flaw.

Remember, just as the yarn runs through your sweater and holds it together, it turns out that in a lot of processes the same performance objectives show up in more than one place. So if you update a performance objective, be sure to update it in every place that it appears in your process. If you don't, your process will come unraveled just as your sweater did when you removed the yarn. Just as the string of yarn holds your sweater together, performance objectives hold your processes together.

Concept

After reading this section you will be able to describe why measuring performance is the key for improving processes. While you are reading this section you will learn about the following aspects of measuring performance.

- Knowledge products have performance objectives.
- Performance objectives support collaborative work.

- Performance objectives provide metrics.
- Performance objectives improve processes.

KNOWLEDGE PRODUCTS HAVE PERFORMANCE OBJECTIVES

In the first four chapters, the product of work was referred to as an *artifact*. That is, it captured the results of people's work. It was also noted that artifacts capture many decisions made during their preparation and hence contain *embedded knowledge*. For example, a quality plan contains embedded knowledge about decisions made during the substep in which the design is *detailed*. In recognition of this embedded knowledge, these products of work are referred to as *knowledge products* throughout the rest of this book. The process diagrammed in Figure 5.1 currently has two performance objectives for the quality plan. To achieve Performance Objective 1, the quality specialist will need to specify the requirements for the product documentation of the paper airplane in the quality plan. To achieve Performance Objective 2, a quality specialist will need to specify the requirements for the life expectancy of the paper airplane in the quality plan. In this book, the term *requirements* will be used to describe the target performance

FIGURE 5.1. IDENTIFYING PERFORMANCE OBJECTIVES FOR KNOWLEDGE PRODUCTS.

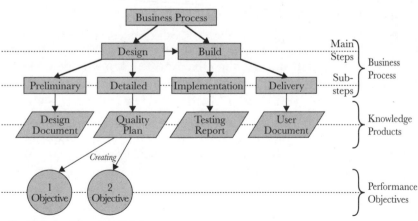

for the final product and the process details to make the product.[1] If the product is a paper airplane, requirements include the language and reading level of the documentation, how much use the airplane can take, and how far it will fly. The term *performance objective* will be used to focus on a specific human performance in completing a knowledge product. Typically, workers address performance objectives by creating product requirements, developing materials to meet the requirements, and measuring those materials against the requirements. A knowledge product typically has several associated performance objectives, each with a stated performance, criterion, and conditions for achieving it. Together, these performance objectives describe what the human worker needs to do to successfully complete a knowledge product, how to determine if the worker did it, and under what conditions it will have to be done. Using performance objectives to describe what knowledge workers will have to do for successfully completing a knowledge product makes it possible to take the next step: identifying the underlying knowledge that a worker will need to know to address the performance objectives in completing the knowledge product. (For a detailed and referenced discussion on improving collaborative work by using performance objectives to develop knowledge products, see my article.[2])

PERFORMANCE OBJECTIVES SUPPORT COLLABORATIVE WORK

The performance objectives that need to be achieved for a knowledge product drive the way that the knowledge product is created. (The diagram in Figure 5.2 illustrates the direct linkage between each performance objective and the knowledge product that addresses it.) So the act of addressing the performance objectives of a knowledge product ultimately determines the knowledge product itself. This means that the work that goes into a knowledge product can be divided up based on the performance objectives. One member of the organization could create Module 1 of a knowledge product to address Performance Objective 1 while another member could create Module 2 to address Performance Objective 2.

FIGURE 5.2. USING PERFORMANCE OBJECTIVES TO SUPPORT COLLABORATIVE WORK.

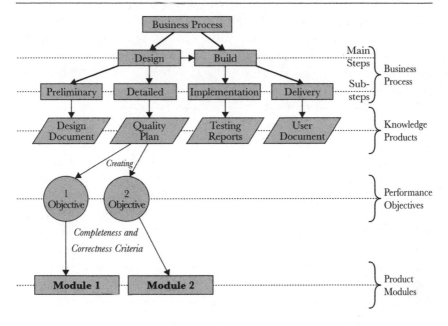

PERFORMANCE OBJECTIVES PROVIDE METRICS

Addressing the performance objectives of a knowledge product is the basis for creating metrics that measure the work of the organization. (Figure 5.3 illustrates this data collection.) Useful metrics go far beyond the "gut analysis" done by most workers involved in a process. For many, the data compiled while working a process are along the lines of "hmmmmm . . . this is too long to wait for feedback from a reviewer—it will make my work late." The idea behind using metrics for process improvement is to place measures where they are likely to be important. Analysis of the data collected may then show that completing a knowledge product simply takes too long or that too much time elapses between the delivery of one knowledge product and the beginning of work on another. Some evaluation data may also show that a certain knowledge product is not at the level of desired quality. Although these findings may have been suspected before measures were in

FIGURE 5.3. USING PERFORMANCE OBJECTIVES TO PROVIDE METRICS.

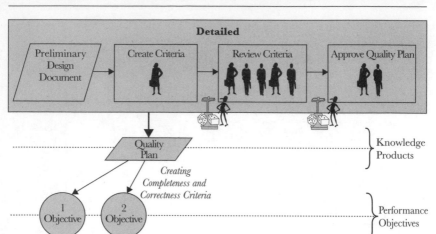

place, the data collected and analyzed from those measures are what allow recommendations to be formed for improvements in the process.

Once a "problem" with a knowledge product is identified, the performance objectives for that knowledge product can provide additional clues for improving the product. Using performance objectives, organizations can ask questions such as, How long does it take to address Performance Objective 1? and, How well did we address Performance Objective 1?

PERFORMANCE OBJECTIVES IMPROVE PROCESSES

A process is improved by focusing on the performance objectives for the knowledge products of that process. As displayed in Figure 5.4, a process separate from the main process is used to make improvements in the main process. In the scenario depicted in Figure 5.4, the *process improvement process* begins with a *revision request* to add a new and third performance objective to the quality plan that has been created in the detailed substep. Next is the *modify process* step, followed by a step to *revise improvements*. Afterward, an *approve revisions* step is completed, before the process improvement becomes part of the main process.

FIGURE 5.4. USING PERFORMANCE OBJECTIVES TO IMPROVE PROCESSES.

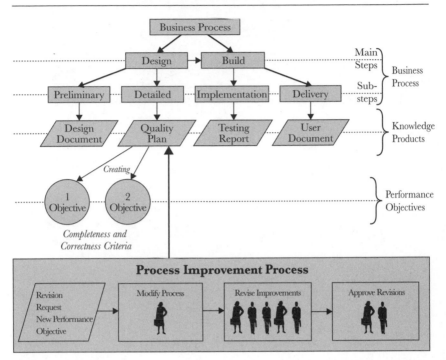

Just as doing the work in the main process requires, the separate process improvement process needs to have an agreed-on way of working and clearly defined roles within that process. In this way, all process improvements are well considered, revised, and approved before becoming part of the main process.

Figure 5.5 shows the result of a process improvement process. A new and third performance objective has been added to the creation of the quality plan in the detailed substep of the design process. In the McBoe Company example, Performance Objective 3 addresses additional product requirements for the new paper airplane—how far it will fly.

APPLICATION

After reading this section you will be able to describe how to measure performance for improving processes in your organization.

FIGURE 5.5. PROCESS IMPROVEMENT RESULT.

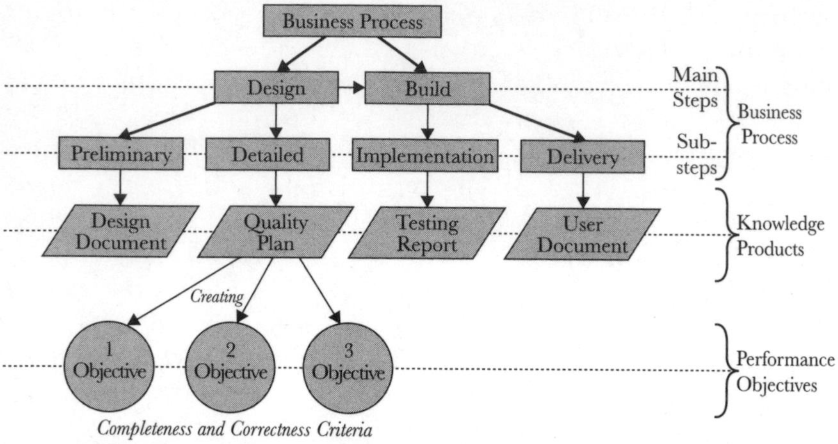

While you are reading this section you will learn about the following techniques for improving processes:

- How to identify performance objectives
- How to support collaborative work
- How to provide metrics
- How to improve processes

How to Identify Performance Objectives

McBoe thought it knew what was required for the knowledge products that it produced, but it discovered otherwise. For example, when the process improvement team looked at some of the best examples of a quality plan, team members found plans that appeared very different. So, first, the team members examined the plans for completeness. They began to list the things that a good quality plan should address. They combined a couple of the listings, deleted one or two, and added a couple to come up with a final list of considerations. Then they looked at each plan to determine if it covered all the considerations a good quality plan should address. The process improvement team then excluded two of the examples because they did in fact not cover everything that should be covered in a good quality plan. Next the team listed these considerations as topics and asked this question for each topic: What performance does a person need to achieve to address this topic? Once the performance was identified, it was specified as a performance objective. For example, the topic "life expectancy of the paper airplane" was specified as this performance objective: "State the requirements, criteria, and conditions for the life expectancy of the airplane." (Figure 5.1 depicts two of the performance objectives that the process improvement team identified that relate to creating product requirements for the paper airplane.) The process improvement team found that even though the task of identifying performance objectives for a knowledge product is somewhat tedious, it is a doable task that is somewhat intuitive. (For a complete treatment of writing performance objectives, see *Preparing Instructional Objectives,* by Mager.[3])

Relate to Your Organization. Does your organization have successful examples of each knowledge product? Do these examples cover all the considerations for successful completion? Can you identify those considerations and rewrite them as performance objectives for each knowledge product?

How to Support Collaborative Work

McBoe knew that it had a little trouble with its process for creating a quality plan. After collecting some metrics, it found that a delay was occurring around getting quality plans approved. In talks with the quality plan approvers, it was discovered that the quality plans awaiting approval spent weeks in an approver's e-mail box before being evaluated. When asked why this happened, the approvers all gave the same answer: "Since it takes an hour to review, I just keep putting it off and before you know it, three weeks have gone by." So the McBoe process improvement team decided to break quality plans into modules. The way to break them up was obvious (and is illustrated in Figure 5.2); they were easily broken into modules that addressed one or more of the performance objectives for a quality plan. Now the McBoe process improvement team went back to the approvers and struck a deal. They asked, "If we promise not to send you over twenty minutes worth of work at a time, will you promise to turn it around within seventy-two hours?" This worked like a charm. By breaking the quality plans into three modules—each taking three days to approve—the average time needed to approve a quality plan dropped from thirty-two days to ten days.

Relate to Your Organization. Does your organization have trouble with the time it takes to complete any knowledge products? Can your organization identify where the delays are? Would it help to break the knowledge product into modules to speed its development?

How to Provide Metrics

As discussed earlier, the idea behind metrics goes far beyond the "gut analysis" done by most workers, and this was true of the workers involved in the McBoe Company manufacturing process too. At McBoe, one place where metrics were thought to be important was the time it takes to complete the create requirements criteria and the review requirements criteria steps (see Figure 5.3). Another place thought to be important was the time that elapsed between the completion of the review requirements criteria step and the beginning of the approve quality plan step. Another important measure identified by the process improvement team was the number of times that a knowledge product such as a quality plan *cycles* through the process.

Relate to Your Organization. Has your organization decided what is important to measure in its process? Has it put in ways to measure these important aspects of its process accurately?

How to Improve Processes

Note that the McBoe process improvement team set out to gather data around those aspects of the process the team felt were important and might need improvement. However, it was the analysis of the data gathered around these aspects of the process that suggested improvements to the McBoe manufacturing process. For example, data analysis showed that the create criteria step simply took too long to complete and that the time elapsing before beginning the review criteria step was far too long. Moreover, data analysis showed that the approve quality plan step was rejecting more than two-thirds of the quality plans processed. This implied a quality problem. In light of this finding the McBoe process improvement team asked the following question, What is not working in the review requirements criteria step so that quality plans are not prepared for approval? Note how far this approach to data collection and analysis in the McBoe manufacturing process is from an intuitive "feel" that something may be taking too long.

In summary, the McBoe Company wanted to improve its manufacturing process. In response to this goal, McBoe established a process similar to the one it uses to get the work done but focused on improving that process. In this way, all process improvements are well considered, revised, and approved before becoming an essential part of the McBoe manufacturing process.

Relate to Your Organization. Has your organization set up a separate process to made sure that all process improvements are well considered, revised, and approved before becoming part of your main process?

Notes

1. I believe earlier knowledge management efforts that focused only on the specific requirements of the final product and the process details to make the product have not led to increased productivity for knowledge workers and have opened up such efforts to criticisms of "Taylorism"—managing knowledge workers as factory workers. (Frederick Taylor is credited for using efficiency studies to improve manufacturing processes.) This book takes the position that in order to grow organizational knowledge and make real improvements in knowledge worker productivity, organizations must focus on the knowledge that is needed by workers to make the knowledge products.
2. M. Salisbury, "A Framework for Collaborative Knowledge Creation," *Knowledge Management Research and Practice, 6*(3), Sept. 2008, 214–224.
3. R. Mager, *Preparing Instructional Objectives: A Critical Tool in the Development of Effective Instruction,* 3rd ed. (Atlanta: Center for Effective Performance, 1997).

PART TWO

FACILITATING INNOVATIVE LEARNING

CHAPTER SIX

MAKING KNOWLEDGE VISIBLE

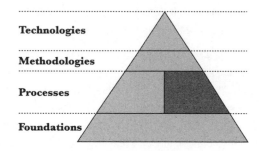

LEARNING OBJECTIVES

After reading this chapter you will be able to do the following:

- *Discuss what* the difference is between explicit and tacit knowledge.
- *Describe why* there is a difference between explicit and tacit knowledge.
- *Describe how* to make knowledge visible in your organization.

EXPERT ADVICE

After reading this section you will be able to discuss what the difference is between explicit and tacit knowledge.

Dear Mark,

My brother-in-law is a blowhard. Last time he was over to our house he kept talking about "tacit" and "explicit" knowledge. Are there such things—or is he just making this up? And if they are real terms, what do they mean so that I can call him on it next time?

Signed, "Tired of Being Fed Baloney"

Dear "Tired of Being Fed Baloney,"

I probably can't help you with your brother-in-law problem. As my dad used to say, "There are people that like to hear themselves talk—whether or not they know anything about what they are talking about." However, we can discuss definitions of these two terms. It turns out that they are related—defining one term helps to define the other. Here's what I mean.

In their 1995 book *The Knowledge-Creating Company,* Nonaka and Takeuchi describe the knowledge transfer process in an organization—beginning with the "tacit knowledge" inside the head of one member in the organization. It's knowledge that is hard to put into words. For example, an experienced insurance claims adjustor may "smell" fraud in a submitted claim but at first might find it difficult to explain why. After examination, the claims adjustor writes in a report that it is a suspicious claim because the insured party just recently increased the fire insurance coverage to an amount that greatly exceeded the value of the insured assets. This documented reason for suspicion in the report becomes "explicit knowledge" that other claims adjustors can internalize—pulling it inside their heads as tacit knowledge for use on the claims for which they are responsible.

Remember this piece of advice for the next time that your brother-in-law is over for a visit and he is rattling on and you can't stand any more. Simply suggest that he should keep the knowledge about that particular subject tacit and to himself.

CONCEPT

After reading this section you will be able to describe why there is a difference between explicit knowledge and tacit knowledge.

While you are reading this section you will learn about the following aspects of making knowledge visible:

- The tacit-explicit-tacit cycle
- Externalization of knowledge
- Internalization of knowledge

THE TACIT-EXPLICIT-TACIT CYCLE

The visibility of knowledge has been examined and discussed by many authors. Generally speaking, it is described in terms of the tacit-explicit-tacit cycle. This cycle begins with the creation of knowledge by a worker in the organization. This knowledge is something that has been learned by the worker but not articulated to others—and perhaps not even consciously known to the worker. So it is "inside" that worker and unknown by others. It is tacit knowledge and invisible to external observers. When that worker "brings it out" and puts it into an explicit form, perhaps by describing it in a document, it becomes explicit knowledge. Now it is knowledge that is visible to others. This explicit knowledge can then be internalized into tacit knowledge by other workers in the organization, who can apply it to their work. Again, it becomes invisible to others, but the results of its successful application convince us that it exists in these workers. However, because it now also exists in an explicit form, more of the organization's knowledge is explicit than it was before this tacit-explicit-tacit cycle existed. In this way an organization can reuse and build on what it knows. (A more thorough description for building this knowledge *spiral* can be found in Nonaka and Takeuchi's 1995 book, *The Knowledge-Creating Company*.[1] The tacit-explicit-tacit cycle presented here is a simpler adaptation of Nonaka and Takeuchi's knowledge spiral that focuses on some workers creating knowledge assets and other workers applying those assets.[2])

EXTERNALIZATION OF KNOWLEDGE

The process of bringing knowledge out in some explicit form in the tacit-explicit-tacit cycle has been studied in the subfield of artificial intelligence known as *knowledge acquisition*.[3] Many of the methods employed for knowledge acquisition use a process that makes use of a template. The goal behind much of this work is to produce methods for subject matter experts to make their tacit knowledge—buried deep inside them—explicit for the rest of the world. However, most of these efforts have resulted in limited success. This reinforces the intuitive notion that it is still a difficult process for individuals to externalize knowledge that resides deep inside them. However, as the tacit-explicit-tacit cycle suggests, if subject matter experts do not externalize what they know, then it cannot be learned and put to use by someone else. The ability to externalize knowledge is a prerequisite for innovative learning in an organization.

Internalization of Knowledge

The other side of the tacit-explicit-tacit cycle has been studied more. This is the process of internalizing explicit knowledge into a tacit form—that, again, resides deep inside a person. We call this process *learning*. A lot of theories to explain human learning have evolved, been adopted, and then cast aside. This history itself emphasizes that learning is not a completely understood process and that it also remains difficult for learners to internalize knowledge so that it becomes tacit and part of them. Like the ability to externalize knowledge, the ability to internalize knowledge is a prerequisite for innovative learning in an organization.

All of this means that designers of systems that support innovative learning must develop support for both sides of the tacit-explicit-tacit cycle. There must be support for acquiring knowledge from subject matter experts and support for the learners of that knowledge.

Application

After reading this section you will be able to describe how to make knowledge visible in your organization. While you are reading this section you will learn the following techniques for increasing the visibility of knowledge:

- How to identify tacit-explicit-tacit cycles
- How to externalize knowledge
- How to internalize knowledge

How to Identify Tacit-Explicit-Tacit Cycles

The knowledge product creation process that was outlined in Figure 5.1 (Chapter Five) involves a tacit-explicit-tacit cycle. For example, during the detailed design step at the McBoe paper airplane company, a quality specialist is likely to have the "makings" for a quality plan in mind even though he or she hasn't written it yet. So the knowledge for the quality plan exists, but it is tacit and invisible to other McBoe workers. The quality specialist then brings the knowledge out in an explicit form when he or she writes the quality plan. After that this knowledge is quite visible to others. This explicit form can then be internalized into tacit knowledge by the people who use the quality plan in their work. Again, their internalized knowledge is invisible to others, but the results of its successful application convince McBoe workers that it exists. For example, even though McBoe workers can't see into the head of the testing specialist, they can observe the well-written testing report that is based on the quality plan. And because the quality plan is written and now exists in an explicit form, more of the organization's knowledge is explicit than it was before this tacit-explicit-tacit cycle—when it was just in the head of the quality specialist.

Relate to Your Organization. In your organization, is it easy to identify the tacit-explicit-tacit cycle for each knowledge product? After a knowledge product is published, is it obvious that the explicit knowledge that is now visible is being applied to the creation of another knowledge product downstream in the business process?

How to Externalize Knowledge

Last year at McBoe, quality plans were found to be inconsistent in their scope and depth of coverage. McBoe set about addressing this problem by requiring quality specialists to use a template with the proper headings as they wrote new quality plans. McBoe also instituted the use of a *performance objectives checklist* to ensure that all quality plans addressed the agreed-upon performance objectives for a quality plan. And finally, McBoe made examples of good quality plans available to its quality specialists. The template, performance objectives checklist, and example plans are now used to "organize" each quality specialist's thoughts into well-written plans that are comprehensive and that have a common format. However, McBoe has found it needs to train new quality specialists in using the template and performance objectives checklist—even when they are workers with previous quality program experience.

McBoe found that poorly written quality plans were an indication that individuals might be having trouble externalizing knowledge that resides deep inside them. McBoe solved the problem by standardizing and improving the process of writing quality plans.

Relate to Your Organization. Are there any poorly made knowledge products in your organization? Could these knowledge products be improved by standardizing and improving the process for creating them?

How to Internalize Knowledge

At McBoe the problem with poor quality plans also created a flip-side problem of poor internalization of knowledge by testing specialists, and this resulted in poor testing reports. In other words, the testing specialists wrote poor testing reports because they used inadequate quality plans to write them. As a result, the testing reports were also inconsistent in their scope and depth of coverage.

McBoe fixed the testing report problem when it fixed the quality plan problem. Once better quality plans became available to the testing specialists, they began writing better testing reports.

Relate to Your Organization. Again, are there any poorly made knowledge products in your organization? Are the poorly made knowledge products affecting the development of other knowledge products downstream in your organization's process?

Notes
1. I. Nonaka and H. Takeuchi, *The Knowledge-Creating Company* (New York: Oxford University Press, 1995).
2. Nonaka and Takeuchi theorize that knowledge is created in evolutionary stages through personal discovery, shared understanding, combining/reusing, and researching. In personal discovery

there is a tacit-to-tacit exchange as a person develops understanding through experience, such as writing a quality plan. Shared understanding is a tacit-to-explicit exchange, such as presenting a quality plan to another person. Combining/reusing is an explicit-to-explicit exchange; swapping quality plans is an example of this. And researching is seeking or absorbing information in the public sector, by examining quality plans provided by a professional society for example.

3. For an overview of the field of knowledge acquisition, see B. Buchanan and D. Wilkins (eds.), *Readings in Knowledge Acquisition and Learning: Automating the Construction and Improvement of Expert Systems* (San Mateo, Calif.: M. Kaufmann, 1992).

CHAPTER SEVEN

DIFFERENTIATING KNOWLEDGE

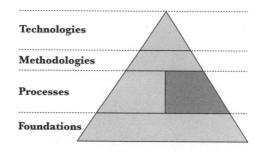

Technologies

Methodologies

Processes

Foundations

LEARNING OBJECTIVES

After reading this chapter you will be able to do the following:

- *Discuss when* there are benefits to categorizing knowledge into different types.
- *Describe why* the four types of knowledge are different.
- *Describe how* to identify the four types of knowledge in your organization.

EXPERT ADVICE

After reading this section you will be able to discuss when there are benefits to categorizing knowledge into different types.

Dear Mark,

What is all this talk about different kinds of knowledge? I've heard of "factual knowledge," "procedural knowledge," "declarative knowledge," and several others. Knowledge is knowledge—right? Isn't this about some academics filling up journals to get publications on their résumés?

Signed, "A Rose by Any Other Name"

Dear "A Rose by Any Other Name,"

I will be the first to admit that all these definitions of knowledge do at first seem confusing and non-value-added. However, recognizing different types of knowledge can help you in designing more supportive computer systems for your organization.

I like the way that Lorin Anderson and David Krathwohl have defined different types of knowledge. They list four distinct types of knowledge: factual, conceptual, procedural, and metacognitive. Factual knowledge is terminology, specific details, and elements. Conceptual knowledge relates to theories, models, principles, and generalizations. Procedural knowledge involves skills, algorithms, and techniques. If you want to impress people at parties, then talk about metacognitive knowledge. It is *knowledge about knowledge* and involves general strategies for learning, thinking, and problem solving. The *heuristics* and *rules of thumb* that experts use to solve problems are metacognitive knowledge.

Remember, organize your computer system so that members of your organization can easily find the type of knowledge that they need. For example, a newcomer to your organization would want access to conceptual knowledge to understand what to do and why. An experienced person may need access primarily to procedural knowledge, in order to follow the steps for completing a process. It's true; different people need different types of knowledge.

CONCEPT

After reading this section you will be able to describe why the four types of knowledge are different. While you are reading this section you will learn about the following aspects of knowledge:

- Knowledge is factual.
- Knowledge is conceptual.
- Knowledge is procedural.
- Knowledge is metacognitive.

Figure 7.1 shows the four types of knowledge named by Anderson and Krathwohl[1] in their revision of Bloom's *Taxonomy of Educational Objectives*.[2] Distinguishing the types of knowledge more clearly and adding one type was one of the major revisions offered by Anderson and Krathwohl. (David Krathwohl wrote a concise overview of this revision to Bloom's taxonomy in an article.[3])

KNOWLEDGE IS FACTUAL

Factual knowledge is described as terminology, specific details, and elements. It's the stuff that "stays the same" (or changes infrequently). It's also the type of thing organizations want to write down—like the steps in a process, or the size of the hole that should be cut into a part, or the length of time a painted part should dry before being used for assembly.

KNOWLEDGE IS CONCEPTUAL

Conceptual knowledge is found in theories, models, principles, and generalizations. The general principles at work in a domain

FIGURE 7.1. THE FOUR TYPES OF KNOWLEDGE.

Metacognitive

Procedural

Conceptual

Factual

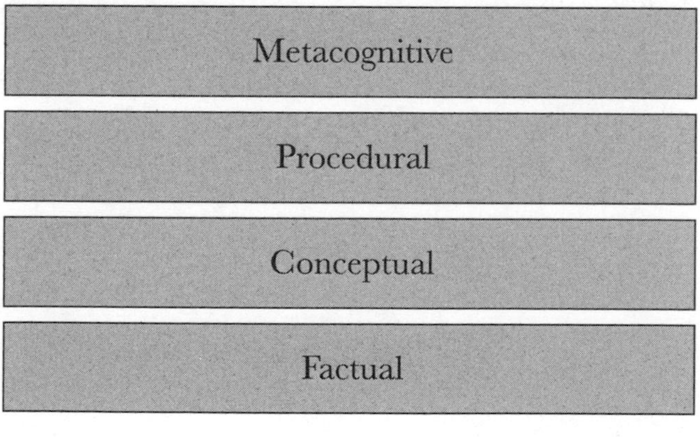

are conceptual knowledge. For airplanes, the conceptual knowledge that matters describes the general principles of aerodynamics that create lift and the ability to steer. These general principles must be followed to create a successful aircraft product.

Knowledge Is Procedural

Procedural knowledge involves skills, algorithms, techniques, and other methods that are specific to a product or process. This is the application of factual and conceptual knowledge to a specific problem. Typically, this knowledge is a step-by-step procedure. It is the how-do-you-do-it knowledge that really puts theory into practice.

Knowledge Is Metacognitive

Metacognitive knowledge was added by Anderson and Krathwohl to Bloom's taxonomy. It is *knowledge about knowledge* and involves general strategies for learning, thinking, and problem solving. Metacognitive knowledge also includes knowledge concerning the appropriate contexts and conditions for the use of the strategies themselves. Additionally, it includes the *heuristics* and *rules of thumb* that experts use to solve problems. In the field of artificial intelligence, this kind of knowledge has been referred to as *metaknowledge.*

Application

After reading this section you will be able to describe how to identify the four types of knowledge used in your organization. While you are reading this section you will learn to do the following:

- How to identify factual knowledge
- How to identify conceptual knowledge
- How to identify procedural knowledge
- How to identify metacognitive knowledge

How to Identify Factual Knowledge

The McBoe Company looked at its manufacturing process to identify the factual knowledge used for the production of paper airplanes. McBoe found that it had an astounding number of terms, specific details, and elements that directly related to its manufacturing process. Although most of this factual knowledge was recorded in manuals, some of it was not. This unrecorded "stuff" was way too much for any one person to commit to memory.

Relate to Your Organization. Are there an astounding number of terms, specific details, and elements that are directly related to the business process in your organization? Is there unrecorded "stuff" that is way too much for any one person to commit to memory?

How to Identify Conceptual Knowledge

When McBoe looked at its manufacturing process for conceptual knowledge, it again found a tremendous number of theories, models, principles, and generalizations that were applied during that process. Although much of it was recorded in materials for training courses, a great deal was not and was just "passed on" from experienced workers to new hires.

Relate to Your Organization. Are there a tremendous number of theories, models, principles, and generalizations that are applied during your organization's process? Is a great deal of this knowledge simply passed on from your experienced workers to new hires.

How to Identify Procedural Knowledge

When it came to identifying procedural knowledge, McBoe found that it indeed had quite a few skills, algorithms, techniques, and other methods that were specific to its manufacturing process. McBoe also found that some of this knowledge was recorded as examples or best practices. However, it found as well that the vast majority of its lifeblood methods were not recorded. Rather, they were in the heads of the experienced workers and picked up through experience by the new hires.

Relate to Your Organization. Does your organization have quite a few skills, algorithms, techniques, and other methods that are specific to its process? Are the vast majority of these lifeblood methods not recorded?

How to Identify Metacognitive Knowledge

McBoe also found that it did have a considerable amount of knowledge about knowledge that involved general strategies for learning, thinking, and problem solving. In addition it had knowledge concerning the appropriate contexts and conditions for the use of the strategies themselves. And it had many heuristics and rules of thumb that its experts used to solve problems. To the McBoe managers' horror, very little of this information was recorded anywhere. Almost all of it was tacit.

Relate to Your Organization. Does your organization have a considerable amount of knowledge about knowledge that involves general strategies for learning, thinking, and problem solving? How about the contexts and conditions for the use of the strategies themselves? And does your organization have many heuristics and rules of thumb that experts use to solve problems? Is very little of this information recorded anywhere?

Notes

1. L. W. Anderson and D. R. Krathwohl (eds.), *Taxonomy for Learning, Teaching, and Assessing: A Revision of Bloom's Taxonomy of Educational Objectives* (New York: Longman, 1998).
2. B. S. Bloom (ed.), *Taxonomy of Educational Objectives:* Handbook I. *Cognitive Domain* (New York: Longmans, Green, 1956).
3. D. R. Krathwohl, "A Revision of Bloom's Taxonomy: An Overview," *Theory into Practice, 41*(4), November 2002, 212–218.

CHAPTER EIGHT

DIFFERENTIATING KNOWLEDGE ASSETS

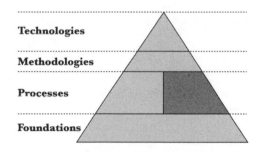

LEARNING OBJECTIVES

After reading this chapter, you will be able to do the following:

- *Discuss when* providing different types of knowledge assets produces benefits.
- *Describe why* knowledge assets provide access to the four different types of knowledge.
- *Describe how* to develop knowledge assets that provide access to the four different types of knowledge in your organization.

EXPERT ADVICE

After reading this section, you will be able to discuss when providing different types of knowledge assets produces benefits.

Dear Mark,

We want to set up our new office computer system so that it is a resource for all our employees—new hires, experienced workers, and our "old-timers." We do have some pretty good classroom training materials with good work examples. Our procedure manuals are up to date and stored in a file cabinet. They also have some good self-study instructional materials. We have a three-ring binder of memos written by our old-timers that provide "tips" on a number of ways to improve what we do and reduce costs. Can you give us a "strategy" for moving these materials to our new computer system?

> *Signed, "Ready to Go—If Only We Knew Where We Were Going"*

Dear "Ready to Go—If Only We Knew Where We Were Going,"

One of the lessons my mom taught me in my early life was to put similar things together so they are easier to find—underwear in the top drawer, socks in the middle drawer—you remember this lesson? Now you need to do the same thing with your materials.

I recommend that you strip out the work examples from your classroom training materials and strip out the self-study instructional materials from the procedural manuals. Next, combine and consolidate your instructional materials to create one online instruction module for each topic.

Now, take all your remaining materials and put them into electronic form. Take the good work examples, list what topic they go with—then take the memos with old-timer tips, and list what topic they go with.

All these materials are *knowledge assets.*

Remember, by organizing your materials by topic, you can create a computer system where it is easy for your new hires to find training on a topic, your experienced workers to find a good work example, and your old-timers to place their tips where people can find them.

CONCEPT

After reading this section you will be able to describe why knowledge assets provide access to the four different types of knowledge.

While you are reading this section you will learn about the following ways to provide access to knowledge:

- Documents embody factual knowledge.
- Instruction embodies conceptual knowledge.
- Examples embody procedural knowledge.
- Expert advice embodies metacognitive knowledge.
- Tacit knowledge should be managed.

DOCUMENTS EMBODY FACTUAL KNOWLEDGE

Documents typically are used to provide access to factual knowledge (Figure 8.1). Although other media forms can be similarly used, documents are probably the best-known and most used medium for capturing and disseminating factual knowledge (that is, terminology, specific details, and elements). Figures 8.1 and 8.2 show how the four types of knowledge relate to the concept of making knowledge visible (explicit), discussed in Chapter Six. For example, the two tones of shading on the "Factual (Documents)" line in Figures 8.1 and 8.2 reflect the reality that most organizations find it desirable to have most of their factual knowledge reside in an explicit form. Figure 8.1 shows where many organizations are now, and Figure 8.2 shows where they could be if they made more of their knowledge explicit. That is, organizations do not want most of their factual knowledge tucked away in the heads of their members. It is better for their work process

FIGURE 8.1. ACCESS TYPICALLY PROVIDED TO THE DIFFERENT TYPES OF KNOWLEDGE.

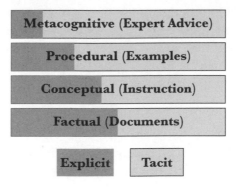

FIGURE 8.2. ACCESS PROVIDED AFTER TACIT KNOWLEDGE IS MADE EXPLICIT.

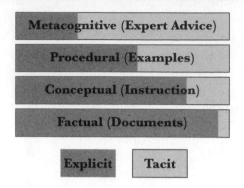

if this knowledge is explicit—written down. Imagine, for example, an organization in which the times for manufacturing processes were not written down anywhere. Workers would just have to try to remember how many minutes and seconds each one should take!

INSTRUCTION EMBODIES CONCEPTUAL KNOWLEDGE

Instruction provides access to conceptual knowledge (Figures 8.1 and 8.2). As with factual knowledge, other resources can provide access to conceptual knowledge, but instruction is the best medium for capturing and disseminating this kind of knowledge (that is, general principles and concepts). Although access to conceptual knowledge may be provided in informal ways, such as individual on-the-job training (Figure 8.1), most organizations will want to make most of their conceptual knowledge explicit (Figure 8.2). This is what is done when new courses are developed. The conceptual knowledge in the heads of an organization's workers is made explicit in the form of course materials. However, we also need to recognize what Figure 8.2 reveals, that not all conceptual knowledge can be made explicit and that organizations will still desire to provide some informal instruction.

EXAMPLES EMBODY PROCEDURAL KNOWLEDGE

Examples provide access to procedural knowledge (Figures 8.1 and 8.2). They describe the step-by-step processes for applying conceptual and factual knowledge to create a unique solution for a specific problem. Although other means can provide access to procedural knowledge, examples are the best medium for this purpose. Figure 8.2 shows the desired level of visible procedural knowledge in an organization. Most organizations will want to make many of their examples of good work explicit so they can provide access to procedural knowledge for their workers. Some of the best examples may become *best practices* for the organization. Nevertheless, it probably will not be possible to write up every example and make the knowledge that went into that example explicit. So a comparatively large amount of an organization's procedural knowledge will remain tacit.

Expert Advice Embodies Metacognitive Knowledge

Expert advice provides access to metacognitive knowledge (Figures 8.1 and 8.2). As knowledge about knowledge, it is used by experts to identify whether a solution is possible and the process with which to solve a difficult problem. Again, although other means can be used to provide access to metacognitive knowledge, expert advice is the oldest, most direct, and accepted means for accessing this kind of knowledge.

Organizations will want to make some of the "gems" of expert advice explicit for all the workers of the organization. However, given today's understanding of cognition and level of technological advancement, we now know that it is not possible to make all metacognitive knowledge in an organization explicit and that most of it, as Figure 8.2 shows, will remain tacit. Those of you who remember the high expectations for *expert systems* during the 1980s will recall that sophisticated and intelligent systems were predicted to be just around the corner. The promise of capturing the human ability to reason in a computer program seemed about to be realized. That just-around-the-corner scenario, of course, didn't play out. Although we have more understanding of human cognition than ever before, we still don't have enough, nor do we have the sophistication to capture that cognition and make it dynamic and responsive. So for the time being, organizations should strive to make some of their gems of metacognitive knowledge explicit—but pick them well, because most metacognitive knowledge in organizations will remain elusive and tacit for the foreseeable future.

Tacit Knowledge Should Be Managed

As noted earlier, Figure 8.2 shows the result of making the four types of knowledge (factual, conceptual, procedural, and metacognitive) more explicit in an organization. Although it is quite an improvement over the situation depicted in Figure 8.1, a question remains, should we "worry" about the fact that a large amount of procedural knowledge and almost all the metacognitive knowledge will remain tacit?

The answer is that even though large amounts of knowledge will remain in the tacit domain even in an organization systematically working to make knowledge more explicit, we can still manage that knowledge. Remember the tacit-explicit-tacit cycle described in Chapter Six? This cycle can take place through the use of an example or nugget of expert advice without a formal process. It can happen through the direct connection between two or more people. For example, a worker may describe the procedure he or she went through to solve a problem to another worker who is working on a similar problem. Or an expert may give some advice to a worker for solving problems with certain characteristics. In both cases the knowledge begins as tacit knowledge in one person. Next it becomes explicit through that person's elaboration. This explicit form is then internalized by a second person and resides as tacit knowledge in that person. Although no knowledge products remain containing the explicit form of the knowledge (no documents, no video, or the like) the tacit-explicit-tacit cycle has been executed. What does this mean for organizations? It means that great amounts of tacit knowledge can be managed through numerous tacit-explicit-tacit cycles involving people in face-to-face settings. The managing comes in when organizations facilitate processes whereby those who need to know something are connected to those who already know it.

However, this doesn't mean connecting people who need to learn to just any kind of knowledge. As we have seen, there are different kinds of knowledge that make up different kinds of knowledge assets. And as you have probably already guessed, there are different kinds of learners looking for these different kinds of knowledge!

Application

After reading this section you will be able to describe how to develop knowledge assets that provide access to the four types of knowledge in your organization. While you are reading this section you will learn about the following methods for creating knowledge assets:

- How to provide access to factual knowledge
- How to provide access to conceptual knowledge
- How to provide access to procedural knowledge
- How to provide access to metacognitive knowledge
- How to manage tacit knowledge

How to Provide Access to Factual Knowledge

The differences between Figure 8.1 and Figure 8.2 in the area of factual knowledge are illustrative of the results of the action that the McBoe Company took to make most of its factual knowledge explicit and to provide access to that knowledge through documents. McBoe formed process teams and documented team processes. Teams used stories to get going on the task (a technique discussed in Chapter Three). They took the results of their initial meetings and finally got agreement on their processes with a review and approval exercise. McBoe took the results of this work to update its manuals. Then, to make it easy for McBoe workers to gain access to those manuals, McBoe put them all on the company intranet.

Relate to Your Organization. Does your organization have updated documents that provide access to the factual knowledge about your processes? Is it easy for your workers to gain access to those documents?

How to Provide Access to Conceptual Knowledge

McBoe also worked to make most of its conceptual knowledge explicit (Figure 8.2) and to provide access to it through instruction. McBoe looked at each task in its process and asked this question: What theories, models, principles, and generalizations are applied to accomplish this task? Then McBoe had instructional designers work with subject matter experts to write small instruction modules for each task. Finally, to make it easy for McBoe workers to access those modules, McBoe put them on the company intranet along with the manuals.

Relate to Your Organization. Does your organization have instruction modules that provide access to the conceptual knowledge about its processes? Is it easy for your workers to access those modules?

How to Provide Access to Procedural Knowledge

As noted in the difference between Figures 8.1 and 8.2, McBoe additionally worked to make more of its procedural knowledge explicit and to provide access to it through examples. McBoe made it a goal to record a good example of how each task was completed. It decided to use small digital video clips to capture these step-by-step examples—each one running around two minutes. McBoe also decided to have its instructional designers shoot the videos and not professional video producers. McBoe's reasoning was that it had to keep the costs down for each example so it could capture examples for the whole manufacturing process. Moreover, it also wanted to follow the philosophy that *knowledge is temporal.* That is, it's going to change. So the recording of it doesn't have to be perfect and expensive—and if it did have to be perfect and expensive, it wouldn't get done in the first place. And in the second place, the examples wouldn't get updated and replaced, because . . . well, they have to be perfect and expensive! And again, to make it easy for McBoe workers to access these examples, McBoe put them on the company intranet along with the manuals and instruction modules.

Relate to Your Organization. Does your organization have examples that provide access to the procedural knowledge about its processes? Is it easy for your workers to gain access to those examples?

HOW TO PROVIDE ACCESS TO METACOGNITIVE KNOWLEDGE

Again as shown in the difference between Figures 8.1 and 8.2, McBoe also worked to make some of its metacognitive knowledge explicit and to provide access to it through expert advice. McBoe decided to capture one good piece of expert advice for each task in its process. It used video to capture this expert advice. And again, because these tidbits of knowledge are, in effect, time stamped, the recording of them needs to be cheap and easy. So once again McBoe made them around two minutes in length and had them filmed by the instructional designers rather than professional video producers. Each piece of expert advice turned out to be a little rule of thumb that took the format "if you do this in this situation, then this will happen." And finally, to make it easy for McBoe workers to access these pieces of expert advice, McBoe put them on the company intranet along with the manuals, instruction modules, and examples.

Relate to Your Organization. Does your organization have captured expert advice that provides access to metacognitive knowledge about its processes? Is it easy for your workers to gain access to this expert advice?

HOW TO MANAGE TACIT KNOWLEDGE

Figure 8.2 shows the result of making the four types of knowledge (factual, conceptual, procedural, and metacognitive) more explicit in the McBoe Company. McBoe did discover as it came out of this process that despite its great efforts to *codify* all its corporate knowledge, a large amount of its procedural knowledge and almost all its metacognitive knowledge still remained tacit in the organization. However, McBoe decided that this was not only an OK situation but actually a preferred one. It decided to manage this knowledge that remained in the tacit dimension by using the tacit-explicit-tacit cycle. It created mechanisms whereby those who needed to know something could be connected to those who knew it. For example, when McBoe wanted to better manage the metacognitive knowledge around creating quality plans, it developed a yellow pages of expert contacts that resided on the company's intranet with the materials associated with the preliminary design step of the manufacturing process. When quality specialists need access to metacognitive knowledge, they can easily locate an expert and gain some expert advice (and McBoe has encouraged this activity with incentives, as described in Chapter Ten). Even though no knowledge assets are generated from these knowledge exchanges, the tacit-explicit-tacit cycle is being executed. At McBoe, a great amount of tacit knowledge is now being managed through numerous tacit-explicit-tacit cycles involving people in face-to-face settings. So even though all this knowledge is not codified, it is being managed.

Relate to Your Organization. Does your organization have a yellow pages, a directory, to connect employees to experts who can provide advice? Are there incentives for the experts to provide expertise? Is it easy for your workers to access these experts?

CHAPTER NINE

DIFFERENTIATING LEARNERS

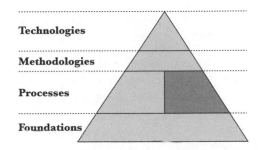

LEARNING OBJECTIVES

After reading this chapter you will be able to do the following:

- *Discuss when* learners have differing cognitive needs.
- *Describe why* learners have differing cognitive needs.
- *Describe how* to meet the cognitive needs for learners in your organization.

EXPERT ADVICE

After reading this section you will be able to discuss when learners have differing cognitive needs.

Dear Mark,

Last year I heard you speak at our brown bag luncheon series. In your talk, you mentioned that training for newcomers, improving performance for experienced workers, and increasing innovation

*for experts were related problems. Since it has been a year, my
notes don't make much sense anymore. Could you explain
this again?*

Signed, "Asking for an Instant Replay"

Dear "Asking for an Instant Replay,"

I have found that most organizations subscribe to the big bang theory of training. That is, once the newcomers have been trained, they are good for life! Sometimes, the big bang theory is still employed, in a modified form, when the needs of the organization change. For example, when the performance of experienced members of the organization isn't up to snuff, the action is to "retrain them," so they can work harder.

If you view increased productivity as a result of continuous and ongoing learning, then the big bang theory doesn't hold up very well. Those newcomers that you once trained don't need more training, but they do need access to good examples of work by other experienced workers. And getting more out of your experts doesn't mean having them work faster and harder but having them take some of their time to share what they know with your newcomers and experienced people. Plan for your experts to continue to learn and give expert advice to the others—thereby boosting the output of everyone in your organization.

Remember that the old sixties rock group The Byrds had it right—"there is a season" for everything,[1] including training for your newcomers. But in the long run, those newcomers won't be new anymore and increased productivity will come only from continuous learning.

CONCEPT

After reading this section you will be able to describe why learners have differing cognitive needs. While you are reading this section you will learn about the following aspects of the cognitive needs of learners:

- Novices understand and remember knowledge.
- Practitioners analyze and apply knowledge.

- Experts create and evaluate knowledge.
- Learners have cognitive needs.

As discussed in Chapter Seven, when Anderson and Krathwohl revised Bloom's taxonomy,[2] they made knowledge a separate dimension with four categories: factual, conceptual, procedural, and metacognitive. In addition, Anderson and Krathwohl assigned Bloom's other categories to a *process dimension,* which describes the learner's cognitive process when solving a problem in each category. And they renamed these categories: Bloom's *knowledge, comprehension, application, analysis, synthesis,* and *evaluation* became *remember, understand, apply, analyze, evaluate,* and *create* (see Figure 9.1). Both these lists are in ascending order. Note that Anderson and Krathwohl place *create* as the highest level of cognition; it describes individuals putting elements together to form a novel coherent whole or make an original product.

NOVICES UNDERSTAND AND REMEMBER KNOWLEDGE

As Figure 9.1 shows, novices are usually working at the level of trying to understand and remember. This is why it takes novices

FIGURE 9.1. LEARNERS HAVE DIFFERING COGNITIVE NEEDS.

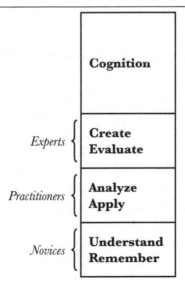

so long to get anything done. They are "stuck" at the level of just trying to get what's going on and put it into memory.

Practitioners Analyze and Apply Knowledge

Practitioners are usually working at the level of analyzing the situation and applying knowledge to form a solution (Figure 9.1). They already understand what to do and remember how to do it. Give them a problem similar to one that they have solved before and they will quickly analyze the problem and take a previous solution, adapt it, and apply it to their new problem.

Experts Create and Evaluate Knowledge

Finally, experts should be working at the level of evaluating solutions and creating new and unique ones (Figure 9.1). If an organization is using its experts like practitioners—having them do the everyday work—then the organization is not getting the most from its experts. Remember, this is where new thinking comes from. Novices are stuck at figuring out what is going on and practitioners can solve only problems they have seen before—and only in the same old way. If the organization's experts are spending all their time on the work of the day, then the opportunity is lost for better ways to do tomorrow's work.

Learners Have Cognitive Needs

Figure 9.2 illustrates in chart form the appropriate knowledge assets to give to specific types of learners. Of course an appropriate knowledge asset depends on the type of knowledge that they seek. Novices use the system to become practitioners, practitioners use the system to become experts, and experts use the system to create new knowledge. In the process of becoming practitioners, novices seek to understand and remember conceptual knowledge. Instructional materials are appropriate knowledge assets for them as these materials provide access to conceptual knowledge. Note, however, that novices will still require factual knowledge to fully understand and remember the conceptual knowledge—similar to a student's requiring access to a manual to understand the

FIGURE 9.2. MEETING LEARNERS' DIFFERING COGNITIVE NEEDS.

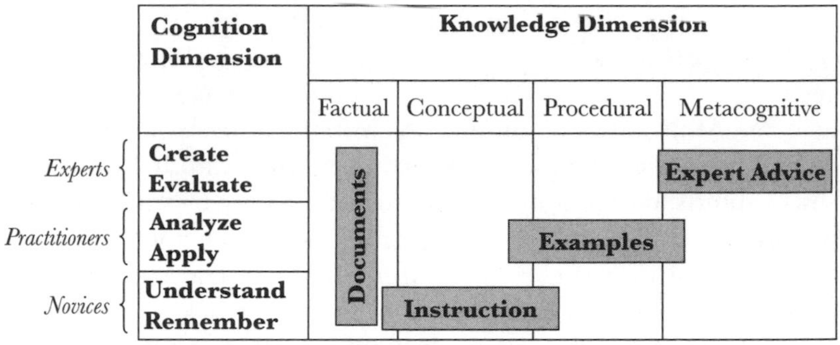

Cognition Dimension	Knowledge Dimension			
	Factual	Conceptual	Procedural	Metacognitive
Experts { **Create** **Evaluate**	Documents			**Expert Advice**
Practitioners { **Analyze** **Apply**			**Examples**	
Novices { **Understand** **Remember**		**Instruction**		

instruction presented in the classroom. In the process of becoming experts, practitioners use examples to analyze and apply procedural knowledge. Note, however, that practitioners will still require factual and conceptual knowledge to apply and analyze procedural knowledge. Experts create and evaluate expert advice. By doing so, they provide access to metacognitive knowledge for others in the organization.

APPLICATION

After reading this section, you will be able to describe how to meet the cognitive needs of learners in your organization. While you are reading this section you will learn about the following ways to meet these cognitive needs:

- How to understand and remember knowledge
- How to analyze and apply knowledge
- How to create and evaluate knowledge
- How to meet learners' cognitive needs

HOW TO UNDERSTAND AND REMEMBER KNOWLEDGE

Two years ago, McBoe identified through a human resource survey that many newly hired employees felt poorly prepared to get their jobs done in a timely and satisfactory manner. Follow-up interviews revealed that many employees reported a "steep learning curve," with a lot of time spent "spinning their wheels." These results were confirmed when McBoe management ran production reports and found that new hires really did take three times as long as experienced employees to get the work done—and that they made twice as many mistakes as their experienced counterparts did. McBoe management was initially at a loss as to what to do. McBoe already had a two-day training program for most of its jobs. A needs assessment was performed to try to understand if this perceived gap existed and, if it did, what the root cause was. McBoe found that there was a breakdown in transferring what employees learned in the classroom to their work at their office desks. As one new hire put it, "Everything made perfect sense in class, but by the time I got back to my desk, I couldn't remember why we were supposed to do some things—and consequently forgot to do them." To close this performance gap, McBoe changed its two-day training classes to include opportunities for employees to apply what they learned in a simulated manufacturing process environment. Even more important, McBoe put small, refresher instruction modules on its intranet, making them accessible to employees at their desks. These small, quick modules moved employees past being stuck at the level of just trying to get what is going on and put it into memory. When McBoe ran production reports after these changes, it found that the new hires now only took one and one-half times as long as their experienced counterparts did to do the work and made only slightly more mistakes. This was a tremendous improvement over the previous situation.

Relate to Your Organization. Do the new hires in your organization have a steep learning curve and spend a lot of their time spinning their wheels? Could they benefit from small, refresher instruction modules accessible through your organization's intranet?

How to Analyze and Apply Knowledge

In that same survey two years ago, McBoe also identified that the experienced employees felt they were "underproducing." Indeed, follow-up interviews revealed that McBoe's experienced employees felt they were "reinventing the wheel" and were not all following "best practices" for each step in the manufacturing process. As with the new hires, McBoe management was initially at a loss as to what to do—if anything. After all, production reports showed that the experienced workers were actually doing the work in less time with fewer mistakes than in the past. McBoe decided to expand the initial needs assessment to look further at this problem. Management wanted to know if a performance problem existed and if there was a root cause. Surprisingly, the needs assessment showed that even though experienced workers shared the same physical space, they shared little about their work. In other words, they worked next to one another but with each one doing his or her own work in his or her own way. The way each did a job was the only way he or she knew to get it done. Looking across all the steps of production, McBoe estimated that if it could get each worker to use the best practice for getting his or her work done, it would shave 20 percent off production time and result in 10 percent fewer defects.

To close this perceived performance gap, McBoe instituted a best practices campaign. For each knowledge product created in the McBoe manufacturing process, McBoe sought to gather good examples, select the best one, and post it on McBoe's intranet. To conduct this campaign, McBoe created a separate process to select the best practices. The roles in this process included the submitters (authors), the reviewers, and the approvers. After successfully populating its intranet with a best practice for each knowledge product, McBoe left the best practice identification process in place. Now, it could update a best practice with a better one after it was run through the best practice process. In this way McBoe used the best practice process both to get a jump start on using best practices and to continue to improve its main process as new best practices were discovered.

It turned out that the projected improvements came close to being realized. As a result of the best practices campaign, McBoe realized an 18 percent decrease in production time and 9 percent reduction in defects.

Relate to Your Organization. Do the experienced workers in your organization feel that they are reinventing the wheel and are not all following best practices for each task?" Could they benefit from a best practices campaign that would populate the organization's intranet with a best practice for each knowledge product?

How to Create and Evaluate Knowledge

While performance problems were being addressed for new hires and experienced workers, a few managers at McBoe were wondering if McBoe was really getting the most from its experts. These highly skilled workers made up only 3 percent of the workforce but took home 8 percent of the payroll. They were a small but significant population of employees and were deemed a valuable company asset.

In expanding the needs assessment conducted with the new hires and the experienced workers to the experts, McBoe management wanted to find out what the experts were really doing. These people received the highest pay because the assumption had always been that their years of experience and a substantial company investment in their continuing professional development made them very productive and a company asset. A survey and follow-up interviews showed what many in management had already suspected. The experts were a company asset; as a group they had extensive knowledge of not only McBoe's manufacturing process but also the trends in the industry. However, they were not any more productive than the experienced employees. And they were spending 95 percent of their day doing work essentially the same as the experienced employees' work. In other words, McBoe was paying the experts mostly to do the same work as everyone else. And because they were paid substantially more than the other workers, they increased production costs—not decreased them as was the assumption before the needs assessment.

"What to do?" thought McBoe managers. "We can't just fire them—but we could let them die out as they retire," said one manager as he was eating a doughnut. What to do indeed! Then, inspired by their success in closing the performance gaps with the new hires and the experienced workers, the managers struck upon this idea: "How about not trying to get 'more' out of our experts but rather something different." And different it was. In light of its successful best practices campaign, McBoe set forth to conduct an expert advice campaign.

In this campaign, McBoe sought to gather good advice for creating each knowledge product, select the best pieces of advice, and post them on the McBoe intranet. And learning from the success of its best practices campaign, McBoe created a separate process to select the best advice. As before, the roles included submitters (authors), reviewers, and approvers. And again, McBoe left the process in place, so it could update the expert advice with better advice after it was run through the expert advice process. As with best practices, McBoe used the expert advice process both to get a jump start on using better expert advice and to continue to improve the process as better advice was developed.

As a result of the expert advice campaign, McBoe experts were now evaluating current advice for each knowledge product in the manufacturing process that explained what actions should be performed under certain conditions. When this evaluation found the current advice lacking, then the experts would go about creating new advice for that knowledge product.

As a way to manage the tacit knowledge of the manufacturing process at McBoe, the experts were also asked to be an *asset* to the other employees. In the system's instructional materials, best practices, and expert advice that were made available for every step in the McBoe manufacturing process, there was also a link to an expert for each step. The experts were trained to understand what kind of knowledge other workers would be seeking from them. That is, they were trained on how novices understand and remember knowledge, how practitioners analyze and apply knowledge, and how experts create and evaluate knowledge. That way, when an expert was contacted by another employee in the organization, he or she would first try to establish "where that learner was coming from" in order to help that learner get done what he or she was trying to do. Acting as an asset was quite a change in perspective for most of the experts. Before, they had viewed giving advice as something they did for free—to friends—so they had tended to guard against spending too much of their time on this "gabbing around the cracker barrel" and had instead made sure they got enough "work" done for the day.

When McBoe started looking at getting more out of its experts, it didn't really know what that would mean. However, as a result of the expert advice campaign, experts now spend 75 percent of their time on production activities, 15 percent on writing expert advice, and 10 percent on offering advice to other employees at McBoe. That has translated into a 5 percent decrease in production time and 10 percent reduction in defects for the entire manufacturing process. Now, after a little calculation, McBoe management agrees that the extra compensation the experts receive is well earned.

Relate to Your Organization. Does management in your organization know what the organization's experts are really doing? Is your organization paying its experts more to do the same work as everyone else? Could your organization benefit from an expert advice campaign that would populate its intranet with expert advice for each knowledge product?

How to Meet Learners' Cognitive Needs

McBoe's efforts to ensure that the cognitive needs of all its learners were met resulted in a system like the one outlined in Figure 9.2. Novices use the system to become practitioners. By interviewing new hires in a follow-up evaluation, McBoe found that the average time it took new hires to feel that they knew their job thoroughly enough to do it as well as the experienced people had shrunk from three months to one and one-half months. Similarly, practitioners used the system to become experts. McBoe's follow-up evaluation showed that practitioners who became experts while using the system reported that they felt they were at the level of expert after one year whereas the older experts who had not had the use of such a system reported that it had taken them three years on average to become an expert. The system was so successful for the McBoe Company because in the process of becoming practitioners, novices could easily access instructional materials and were able to understand and remember these materials. The instructional materials gave them access to conceptual knowledge. Practitioners went through a similar process. They easily accessed best practices from the system, and these practices gave them access to procedural knowledge. Furthermore, McBoe's experts now spend more of their time in writing expert advice. In the follow-up survey the experts reported that their main reason for changing their work habits was to make their efforts more aligned with McBoe management expectations. However, the experts also reported that having a system that made it easy to submit, review, approve, and publish the advice was also important to them. They could now easily see the fruits of their work—and the work of other experts. Now giving advice was no longer seen as something they did for free. The experts were now being paid for their expertise—and not just for the work they did (which was like the work of the practitioners). And the system also helped to make the experts part of the *network* at McBoe for managing the tacit knowledge around the manufacturing process. When contacted for advice, the experts easily agreed to share what they knew and proudly recorded the time on their time cards.

Relate to Your Organization. Does your organization have a systematic way to ensure that the cognitive needs of all its learners are met? Do its new hires have easy access to instructional materials? Do its practitioners have easy access to best practices? And do its experts see that their advice is easily accessed and used?

Notes
1. These words come almost verbatim from the King James version of the Bible (Ecclesiastes 3, verses 1–8) and were turned into a song by Pete Seeger; see, for example, http://en.wikipedia.org/wiki/Turn!_Turn!_Turn!_(to_Everything_There_Is_a_Season).
2. L. W. Anderson and D. R. Krathwohl (eds.), *Taxonomy for Learning, Teaching, and Assessing: A Revision of Bloom's Taxonomy of Educational Objectives* (New York: Longman, 1998).

PART THREE

ENABLING AN iLEARNING ORGANIZATION

CHAPTER TEN

LOCATING AND MARSHALING EXPERTISE

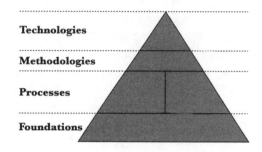

LEARNING OBJECTIVES

After reading this chapter you will be able to do the following:

- *Discuss when* social network analysis is useful for locating and marshaling expertise in organizations.
- *Describe why* social network analysis is useful for locating and marshaling expertise in organizations.
- *Describe how* to use social network analysis to locate and marshal expertise in your organization.

EXPERT ADVICE

After reading this section you will be able to discuss when social network analysis is useful for locating and marshaling expertise in organizations.

Dear Mark,

Three months ago we put up a Web site for our small nondenominational church. One of our goals was to have a place on the Web site where members of our church could find out who is in the hospital and how they are doing. However, as most of us know, hospitals do not give out such information anymore. How can we accomplish this goal and supply this information to our congregation?

Signed, "Kept in the Dark"

Dear "Kept in the Dark,"

When I was growing up, we had a woman in our small rural community who knew everything about everyone. As one of the townspeople put it, "She's the most nosy person I've ever known—but in a good way." She knew the people who were sick, why they were sick, how long they were sick, and the contents of their doctor's written report. So, if you wanted to know how someone was doing without disturbing his or her family, all you had to do was give Loretta a call. On more than one level she really provided a service to the community. Many fundraisers for families in need could be traced back to the "news reporting" of Loretta.

In big organizations a new method for finding the people in the know like Loretta is called *social network analysis,* or SNA for short. The concept is to find those people in an organization who pass on information to those who need it. However, I suspect your church is small enough that you will be able to find your Loretta without much effort. Once found, convince her to take on the job of supplying your Web site with the needed information.

Remember, don't allow your Loretta to say no. Social network analysis tells us that she does this naturally. So her only reservations might be about using the Web site, which you can remedy by training her—or by making arrangements to upload her information for her.

CONCEPT

After reading this section you will be able to describe why social network analysis is useful for locating and marshaling expertise in organizations. While you are reading this section you will learn about the following aspects of social network analysis:

- Using social network analysis to locate expertise
- Marshaling expertise to produce knowledge assets

Using Social Network Analysis to Locate Expertise

Figure 10.1 shows the result of using social network analysis (SNA) to identify the knowledge flows in an organization. It seeks to answer the question, from whom do people seek information and knowledge? As Figure 10.1 shows, sometimes the people who are sought are internal to an organization, and sometimes they are external. Note that whereas an organizational chart shows formal relationships—who works where and who reports to whom—a social network analysis chart shows informal relationships—who knows whom and who shares information and knowledge with whom.

Implicit in the question of from whom people seek information and knowledge is the element of from trust. That is, the question could also be asked this way: Whose information and knowledge do people trust?

The process of social network analysis typically involves the use of questionnaires and sometimes interviews to gather information about the relationships within a group of people. Sometimes the responses gathered are then mapped using a software tool specifically designed for the purpose.

Figure 10.1. Using Social Network Analysis to Locate Expertise.

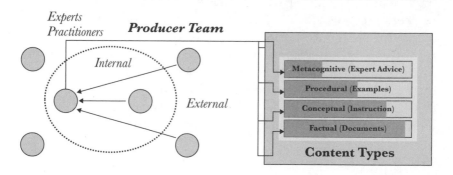

The results can be reported in a chart (as seen in Figure 10.1). Typically, this is the result of analyzing a small group with a simple set of questions. Charts such as this can reveal individuals with trusted expertise as well as individuals who are isolated from the rest of the group. Charts can also show any bottlenecks for information flow that might exist. These results can be used to select interventions that address bottlenecks and identify trusted sources for developing knowledge assets.

Sometimes, for more reporting of more complex results, tables are constructed that indicate the number of individuals, their relationships, and the strength of the relationships. This sort of reporting can reveal the overall breadth and depth of *networking* in an organization. These results can be used to select interventions that are aimed at improving information flow across the organization. (Cross and Prusak provide a useful overview of social network analysis.[1] They introduce the idea of SNA with a simple example and terminology.[2])

MARSHALING EXPERTISE TO PRODUCE KNOWLEDGE ASSETS

Figure 10.1 also shows the results of social network analysis being used to form a knowledge asset "producer team." Typically, these producer teams are made up of the individuals who provide the most trusted expertise for a certain topic in the organization. Usually, these individuals are practitioners or experts in the topic area. Keep in mind that these are the people who are the go-to individuals for knowledge on a certain topic. They are trusted, and their knowledge is used in the production processes of the organization. But all the communication they have had with other workers previously has been informal. Now, once they are identified through social network analysis, they become the desired resources for the development of trusted knowledge assets for the organization. They are already providing much of their knowledge informally; now they are being asked to do it formally. That is, they are being asked to become part of a *knowledge asset producer team* and to assist in developing documents, tutorials, examples, or expert advice.

Application

After reading this section you will be able to describe how to use social network analysis to locate and marshal expertise in your organization. While you are reading this section you will learn about the following two techniques:

- How to use social network analysis to locate expertise
- How to marshal expertise to produce knowledge assets

How to Use Social Network Analysis to Locate Expertise

After the McBoe Company conducted an extensive needs assessment and learned that it needed to create different kinds of knowledge assets (documents, tutorials, examples, and expert advice) for its differing learners (novices, practitioners, and experts), the question soon became, Where are these knowledge assets going to come from? Recognizing that well-designed and organized knowledge assets were needed, McBoe set about putting together a team of instructional designers to craft the knowledge assets. But the question remained, now refocused as, Who are the subject matter experts for each knowledge asset? Someone in management had heard of using social network analysis to identify trusted experts in organizations. McBoe decided to give SNA a try.

For each performance objective of a knowledge product, an instructional designer asked a set of structured interview questions of each worker responsible for achieving that performance objective in the McBoe manufacturing process. The questions in the interview were all variations on this basic question: When you need information to address this performance objective, from whom do you seek information and knowledge? After looking at all the interview answers, the instructional designers created a chart like the one in Figure 10.1 for every performance objective to be achieved at McBoe.

The resulting charts revealed the individuals with trusted expertise for each performance objective. It also showed trusted individuals who were outside the immediate group responsible for achieving the performance objective. A couple of charts showed some disturbing bottlenecks for information flow. In analyzing the series of charts for the performance objectives, it was found that one person was the only trusted source for twelve performance objectives that made up two of McBoe's knowledge products! And he was close to retirement age! This was an unexpected benefit that McBoe realized from employing SNA; the company found it had too little redundancy, or overlap, in expertise in some parts of the manufacturing process.

Relate to Your Organization. Does your organization need to create different kinds of knowledge assets (documents, tutorials, examples, and expert advice) for its differing learners (novices, practitioners, and experts)? Does it know where these knowledge assets are going to come from? Does it know who the subject matter experts are for these knowledge assets?

How to Marshal Expertise to Produce Knowledge Assets

McBoe used the results of the SNA to form knowledge asset producer teams. Each team consisted of the individuals who provided the most trusted expertise for a specific performance objective in the manufacturing process. Typically, these individuals were practitioners or experts in achieving the performance objective. One of the issues that McBoe had to overcome was the perception that it was asking team members to take on added responsibility. Previously, these people had been the go-to individuals for knowledge on a certain performance objective. They had already provided much of their knowledge informally; now they were being asked to do it formally. That is, they were being asked to become part of a knowledge asset producer team and to assist in developing documents, tutorials, examples, or expert advice.

McBoe management knew that a message needed to be sent to these knowledge asset producer teams, especially to the experts on these teams. That message needed to say, loudly and clearly, that this new responsibility was not something to get done in one's spare time; rather, it was the most important thing team members could do for the company. To get the message through, McBoe management decided to make participating on the knowledge asset producer teams part of each team member's job—and to pay people for it. McBoe was going to back up the message with incentives. This decision becomes another story in itself and is described in Chapter Eleven.

Relate to Your Organization. Has your organization used the results of an SNA to form knowledge asset producer teams? Do these teams consist of the individuals who provide the most trusted expertise for each performance objective in one of your organization's processes? Has your organization sent the message loud and clear that this new responsibility is not something to get done in one's spare time; rather, it is the most important thing team members can do for your organization?

Notes

1. R. Cross and L. Prusak, "The People That Make Organizations Go—or Stop," *Harvard Business Review,* June 2002, pp. 104–112.
2. Cross and Prusak discuss the different categories of participants in social networks. They present *central connectors* who link people in their own network with others within that network. *Boundary spanners* are people who manage to connect their own informal network with other networks within the company. *Information brokers* keep the subgroups within a network together and connected. *Peripheral specialists* are the people to turn to for specialized expertise.

CHAPTER ELEVEN

ENSURING INCENTIVES TO SHARE

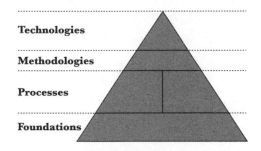

LEARNING OBJECTIVES

After reading this chapter you will be able to do the following:

- *Discuss when* the economic concept of the market explains the dynamics of knowledge sharing in organizations.
- *Describe why* the economic concept of the market explains the dynamics of knowledge sharing in organizations.
- *Describe how* to provide incentives for people in your organization to share their knowledge.

EXPERT ADVICE

After reading this section you will be able to discuss when the economic concept of the market explains the dynamics of knowledge sharing in organizations.

Dear Mark,

I know that we are supposed to be in a "knowledge economy." However, I have recently heard several people in our company mention the term "knowledge markets." It seems to me that they are referring to how people go about exchanging knowledge inside an organization. However, it doesn't entirely make sense to me. Could you clarify what a knowledge market is within the context of an organization?

Signed "In the Market for Knowledge"

Dear "In the Market for Knowledge,"

There is an old saying that goes, "Grace is given of God; but knowledge is bought in the market."[1] I like the definition and description of knowledge markets within organizations offered by Thomas Davenport and Laurence Prusak in their book *Working Knowledge.*[2]

Davenport and Prusak point out that recognizing that knowledge markets exist and that they operate similarly to other markets is key to managing knowledge successfully in an organization. As with other markets, there are buyers, sellers, and brokers. The buyers are looking for insights, judgments, and understanding to help them make better decisions. The sellers are the people in an organization who have a reputation for substantial knowledge about a process or subject. And the brokers are the ones who make connections between buyers and sellers.

Remember, there is a price system in knowledge markets, just as in other markets. This price system has its own "currency" for exchange. Sellers will share knowledge with buyers when they expect the buyers to share too when the sellers are looking for knowledge. Sellers also want repute, especially if it leads to tangible benefits—promotions, bonuses, and the like. And finally, altruism plays a part. Believe it or not, there are individuals who simply like helping—but, as my father used to say, they are few and far between. So don't forget to promote the currency of exchange in your organization's knowledge market.

CONCEPT

After reading this section you will be able to describe why the economic concept of the market explains the dynamics of knowledge sharing in organizations. While you are reading this section you will learn about the following aspects of incentives for sharing:

- People work in their own self-interest.
- Barriers to knowledge sharing need to be removed.
- Hard rewards for knowledge sharing need to be developed.
- Soft rewards for knowledge sharing need to be developed.

PEOPLE WORK IN THEIR OWN SELF-INTEREST

My dad was a logger. He was a timber faller—his job was to cut down trees. That meant he used a power saw to cut down the trees, buck them (trim off the branches), and cut them into logs. Next, a choker setter would take a cable attached to a bulldozer and wrap it around the logs, one at time. The operator of the bulldozer then pulled each log to a landing where it was loaded onto a log truck. Because most of the bulldozers were manufactured by Caterpillar, they were commonly called *cats*. In logging operations the bulldozer operator is considered the most skilled worker and is paid the most. I once asked my dad if he had ever operated a big cat. He responded by telling me his big cat story. It went like this. The men who operated the big cats were in high demand; relatively speaking, there were few men who knew how to operate a big cat. This scarcity of operators, of course, created the situation that led to the high wages for the big cat operators. I interrupted my dad's story by noting that one of his good friends was a big cat operator—why didn't he teach my dad how to drive a big cat? With a twinkle in his eye, my dad went on to explain that even if a big cat operator is your friend, and he agrees to teach you how to drive a cat, and the boss approves it, something, somehow, will come up and the lesson will be postponed and eventually cancelled. The big cat operators just never seem to have an opportunity to teach anyone else how to run the big cats.

The lesson here, of course, is that big cat operators know that their value to their company lies in their ownership of a scarce resource: the ability to operate a bulldozer. Teaching others how to operate a big cat makes the resource less scarce and lowers their bargaining position with the company. It is clearly in the best interest of a big cat operator not to teach anyone else how to operate a big cat.

I know what some of you are thinking. You're getting my point, and you're visualizing a particular coworker sitting on top of a large bulldozer. And some of you who are particularly open and reflective may have noticed that your own desk is starting to look a little like a big cat; sitting before you is work that you are very proud no one else knows how to do.

At one time or another, we have all been trapped by the big cat principle. Keeping our knowledge private and receiving compensation for applying that knowledge reinforces this behavior in all of us. The model that has been reinforced in us is that we are paid for what we do. We need to change our perception of our value to a company; we are paid for the knowledge that we create and share.

This takes us back to a lesson that we should have learned in kindergarten. And that lessen is . . . are you ready for this? It is a good thing to share with others! As illustrated by the big cat principle, this lesson is harder for adults to learn than it is for children. Children, once it is explained to them, readily see the benefit of sharing. They go through a thought process something like this: "When I keep a toy to myself, I get to play with that toy. But when I share my toy with another kid, I will, either now or later, get to play with that kid's toy too. So I get more when I share!"

Unfortunately, the adults of our species require proof that this is indeed the real truth. What has worked well for me in the past is to prove the "sharing is good" concept by explaining it in the context of thirty years of research in social exchange theory. Only by pointing to the work of hundreds of professional social scientists, dressed in lab coats, can it be proven to the average company employee that sharing is indeed good. (See Michener, Lamater, and Myers's textbook, *Social Psychology*, for a good introduction to social exchange theory.[3])

BARRIERS TO KNOWLEDGE SHARING NEED TO BE REMOVED

Before any knowledge sharing can be realized, barriers to knowledge sharing have to be removed. This begins with the organization looking at its process to see whether there are any obvious obstacles at work. For example, for no reason except to save money, perhaps management has three people assigned to each desk. As a group they work around the clock but individually they do not have over-lapping shifts—they never see one another. Although reducing the overhead costs, this situation creates an obstacle to their sharing what they learn on the job. I thought this was an extreme example when I first wrote it—but think about the physical layout of your own office space. Is your organization using a facility configuration that saves a little each month but discourages knowledge sharing? Consider the organization that gets a great deal on a remodeled motel, but workers are tucked into small office areas where they have little interaction with one another. As a result, they end up sharing little with each other—regardless of how inclined they are to share. (Take a look at Thomas Davenport's interesting chapter on the physical work environment and knowledge worker perfor-mance in his book *Thinking for a Living*.[4])

Also, it is very important to determine up front the general health of your organization. That is, you have to verify that the mis-sion makes sense to everyone and is supported by everyone. Like-wise, you have to make sure that the organization has a clear vision of where it is going and that everyone is aligned with that vision. And finally, you have to assess how high the level of trust exists between the members of the organization. A problem in any of these areas jeopardizes the success of any effort to improve sharing. A "sick" organization will not be "cured" with knowledge sharing. So what is important here is to get the organization as healthy as possible so that any knowledge-sharing initiative will "stick" in people's behavior.

HARD REWARDS FOR KNOWLEDGE SHARING NEED TO BE DEVELOPED

Once obvious barriers are out of the way, the type of reward that will be an incentive for sharing should be considered. It's been argued by some that companies should offer outright pay to individuals who share their knowledge. This outright payment might take the form of a raise, stock options, or a bonus. Another *hard* (that is, tangible) reward for sharing knowledge is access to the knowledge contributed by others. The idea to get across here is that "if I give up something that has value, I will get something valuable in return." Yet another hard reward is tying career advancement to the extent that individuals do not hoard but share their expertise. This is a more *holistic* approach than trying to reward each small act of sharing; advancement in the organization is based in part on helping other colleagues perform well. For some organizations, this may be a better way to leverage hard rewards.

SOFT REWARDS FOR KNOWLEDGE SHARING NEED TO BE DEVELOPED

Another reward system involves the review, selection, and development of so-called soft rewards for sharing knowledge. These rewards apply Abraham Maslow's theory of self-actualization.[5] Maslow saw human experience as a quest to satisfy a hierarchy of needs. Beyond the physiological needs for air, water, food, sleep, and sex, he laid out four broad layers: the needs for safety and security, the needs for love and belonging, the need for esteem from others and oneself, and the need to actualize the self, in that order. So, in Maslow's view of human experience, once employees have the basics (food and shelter) they respond only to rewards that help them satisfy higher-level needs such as the need for esteem. Maslow identified two versions of esteem needs, one lower and one higher in the hierarchy. The lower one is the need for the respect of others, for status, fame, glory, recognition, attention, reputation, appreciation, dignity, and even dominance. The higher form involves the need for self-respect, including such feelings as confidence, competence, achievement, mastery, independence, and freedom.

In short, people want more than money for doing their job. Once the basics of food and shelter are met, they look to satisfy higher needs, such as the ones around esteem. This is where the soft rewards come in. One of the soft rewards worth discussing in organizations seeking to have employees share knowledge is enhanced reputation. One reward of this type is acknowledgement from peers for a contribution. Another example is collaboration by a worker of higher status with one of lower status.

Another important soft reward is personal satisfaction. It has been shown that some people gain pleasure simply from demonstrating their own altruistic and prosocial behavior and seeing the results of their efforts.

APPLICATION

After reading this section you will be able to describe how to provide incentives for people in your organization to share their knowledge. While you are reading this section you will learn about the following techniques for developing incentives:

* How to align with people's self-interest
* How to remove barriers
* How to develop hard rewards
* How to develop soft rewards

HOW TO ALIGN WITH PEOPLE'S SELF-INTEREST

The people who work for the McBoe Company are pretty much like other highly skilled engineers and technicians who work in the private sector or government agencies. They are smart, work hard, and wish to be recognized for their efforts. That means that any announcement that instructs them to "share knowledge" will fall on deaf ears. Pronouncement alone does not act as an incentive to follow the instruction to share.

When the McBoe Company was in the process of trying to populate its intranet site with good examples of work, it found it difficult at first to get people to step forward and volunteer their examples. It appeared that two reasons were at work. For one thing, many of the people asked for examples were considered experts in their area of work. They had enjoyed recognition and gratitude for their willingness to help others solve specific problems that reared their ugly heads. When such a problem surfaced, they were "happy to help out" but, unfortunately, were also just too busy to teach anyone else how to do what they did. However, the next time a similar situation arose they would once again be more than "happy to help out." When it was over, invariably, they would again be too busy to teach anyone else how to do what they could do. Recognition was their reward along with a good feeling of being "irreplaceable." Although they were older workers, they did not have to suffer the indignities of worrying about being replaced by younger workers. All they heard was concern about how McBoe would get along without them once they did retire. Why would they want to wreck this situation for themselves? Currently, they were solving difficult problems for McBoe and getting lots of recognition. And it was recognition for years of experience. It made all those years of meetings, report writing, and other less than exciting aspects of work worthwhile. It made their experience worth something. They were deemed a "valuable asset" to McBoe.

Passing along what they knew would ruin this whole favorable situation for these experts. Once the examples were out there on the intranet, then why would any worker ask the experts to solve a problem when that worker could use the example to solve the problem himself or herself? It was obvious. From the experts' perspective, it was clearly not in their self-interest to share what they knew.

So what happened? The expected happened. When the experts were interviewed, they told a completely incoherent story. When describing examples, they jumped around from one reason to another as to why one example should be used over another. "But what example should be used for this step," they were asked. "It depends," they would say. And so it went. Hours and hours went by—no examples were described in sufficient detail to be helpful to anyone.

In a debriefing session, managers contemplated whether the experts had tried to be confusing on purpose. Not so, it was finally agreed. At least not on a conscious level—but perhaps, just maybe, their behavior was rooted in concerns at a subconscious level not even known to them. At the same time, it was known that researchers in the area of knowledge acquisition are painfully aware of the difficulties of getting expertise from subject matter experts. (See Buchanan and Wilkins's book, *Readings in Knowledge Acquisition and Learning,* for an overview of the ways researchers have tried to overcome the difficulties in knowledge acquisition.[6]) So it was concluded that not only was it difficult to get the expertise from these experts but that they were reluctant to divulge what they knew—a reluctance unknown even to them. It was simply not in their self-interest to share what they knew.

Something had to be done to make sharing examples of work in their best interest. But how was McBoe going to do this?

Relate to Your Organization. Do you have people who are smart, work hard, and wish to be recognized for their efforts in your organization? When a directive is given to them to share what they know with coworkers, does it fall on deaf ears? Is your organization looking for a way to make sharing examples of work in these individuals' best interest?

How to Remove Barriers

Before tackling this problem, McBoe took a look at its own general health. Interestingly enough, one of McBoe's major goals in adapting an improved process with a supporting intranet was to achieve its "common vision for creating an iLearning organization." However, this vision was not commonly held by all the employees of the McBoe Company and was unlikely to be commonly held until an improved process with a supporting intranet was rolled out. So McBoe was faced with a Catch-22 situation. Until a common vision of an iLearning organization was accepted and everyone was aligned with that vision, knowledge sharing would be difficult to achieve. However, without knowledge sharing (in this case in the form of examples of work), it would be difficult to realize all the benefits from an improved process with a supporting intranet. So the only choice for McBoe was to move forward as best as it could in capturing and storing work examples for easy retrieval from the intranet site.

Trust was also an issue in developing an improved process with a supporting intranet, because many of the workgroups at McBoe see each other as competitors rather than as partners in the process. McBoe had hoped that the improved process with a supporting intranet would alleviate some of this distrust and make clear which workgroups were responsible for doing what work in McBoe's improved manufacturing process.

Again, this was a Catch-22 situation. Until the workgroups achieved reciprocal trust, it would be difficult for them to achieve knowledge sharing. However, without knowledge sharing, it would be difficult for the workgroups, and McBoe, to realize all the benefits of that improved process and supporting intranet. So, again, McBoe's only choice was to move forward as best as it could in capturing and storing work examples for easy retrieval from the intranet site and to hope that this activity would build the trust needed to continue the work.

Relate to Your Organization. Is a common vision accepted in your organization, and is everyone aligned to that vision? Is there a high amount of distrust in your organization? Do people in your organization need to share knowledge in order to build trust?

How to Develop Hard Rewards

McBoe is somewhat set in its ways, so it was not possible for it to implement a true hard-reward system for sharing knowledge. McBoe has historically had rules for compensation that involve grade, job description, and so on. In other words, outright hard rewards were not part of the McBoe culture. So an immediate payment in the form of a raise or bonus to individuals who share their knowledge was not an option for the McBoe Company at that time. However, McBoe also wanted to send a loud and clear message that sharing knowledge was going to be the new culture at McBoe. So management put into place a policy that tied career advancement to the extent that individuals did not hoard but instead shared their expertise. This measure has become part of individual performance reviews at the same time that the improved manufacturing process and its supporting intranet are becoming accepted. (Some of the details of these changes in individual performance reviews are covered in Chapter Twelve.)

McBoe's new individual performance reviews that address knowledge sharing have turned out to be quite a success. In less than two cycles (two years) the company climate has started to shift to favor knowledge sharing as more junior-level managers who embrace the idea are being identified in performance reviews and are starting to climb the corporate ladder.

Relate to Your Organization. Is it possible to implement a true hard-reward system for sharing knowledge in your organization? If so, is it possible to provide outright payments in the form of a raise or bonus to individuals who share their knowledge? How about tying career advancement to the extent that individuals do not hoard but share their expertise?

HOW TO DEVELOP SOFT REWARDS

Although McBoe looked at hard rewards, the company knew that soft rewards would also have to be part of the answer to the issue of sharing knowledge. Remember, McBoe Company experts are highly compensated individuals, and as Maslow tells us, once employees have the basics (food and shelter), they respond only to rewards that help them satisfy higher-level needs, such as the need for esteem.

By this time, McBoe had made, and failed at, several attempts to get people to share what they know. So when one of the program managers had a successful case of knowledge sharing, McBoe managers were all ears. It happened on another high-visibility project. Experts in one of McBoe's engineering units were asked to be mentors to younger engineers. To make it worthwhile, the engineering unit established a mentor team. Team members were given time and resources to meet off-site. There they exchanged strategies about how best to mentor the young engineers. And of course the mentors were also given time to meet with the young engineers. According to the program manager, this approach was wildly successful because the mentors had been given elevated status. Moreover (and the engineering unit stressed this important point), it was *real* status because it took real budget and approvals from top management to get it done. It cost something. And that was the key. The mentors were also excused from some ordinary work—"Joe won't be at the staff meeting today, he's attending a meeting for the mentor program." Mentoring was then more important than ordinary work. Joe was then more important than ordinary workers.

Maslow's hierarchy was proven right in this case: mentors readily responded to the rewards that helped them satisfy their need for esteem. They particularly responded to Maslow's lower

level of self-esteem—the need for the respect of others, for status, fame, glory, recognition, attention, reputation, appreciation,
dignity, and even dominance. This example explains why simple
awards or pat-on-the-head responses never really work. They don't
cost anything—so they aren't worth anything. One of the great mis-
conceptions about soft rewards is that they are cheaper than hard
rewards. It's true that they can be comparatively less expensive—
but they won't work if they are cheap. People know if this kind of
reward cost something or not. If it cost something, then it's worth
something. If it didn't cost anything, then it's not worth anything.
Give someone a reward that costs something and it raises his or
her self-esteem. Give someone something that doesn't cost anything, and it does nothing for his or her self-esteem.

After learning from this experience in one of its engineering
units, the McBoe Company was successful in creating other soft
rewards that encouraged experts to provide good work examples
for the improved manufacturing process. The experts were given
time and budgets to work on the examples and were sent on trips
to work with instructional designers. As they worked on the examples, coworkers could see them responding to Maslow's higher
level of self-esteem—self-respect, including such feelings as confidence, competence, achievement, mastery, independence, and
freedom. They became much more confident. They didn't have
to keep reviewing examples over and over again as they did when
the program started. And they began to talk about life after retirement from McBoe. They began to talk about being hired back as
highly paid consultants.

Relate to Your Organization. Has your organization had failures
in the past in trying to use soft rewards to get people to share
what they know? If so, was it because the rewards weren't really
rewards—they cost nothing? Would people in your organization
respond to Maslow's lower level of self-esteem—the need for
the respect of others, for status, fame, glory, recognition, attention, reputation, appreciation, dignity, and even dominance—and
share what they know? Would they respond to Maslow's higher
level of self-esteem—self-respect, including such feelings as
confidence, competence, achievement, mastery, independence,
and freedom—would that help them to share knowledge?

Notes

1. Arthur Hugh Clough, English poet (1819–1861).
2. T. Davenport and L. Prusak, *Working Knowledge: How Organizations Manage What They Know* (Boston: Harvard Business School Press, 1998).
3. H. A. Michener, J. D. Lamater, and D. J. Myers, *Social Psychology*, 5th ed. (Belmont, Calif.: Wadsworth/Thompson Learning, 2004).
4. T. Davenport, *Thinking for a Living: How to Get Better Performances and Results from Knowledge Workers* (Boston: Harvard Business School Press, 2005).
5. A. Maslow, *Toward a Psychology of Being*, 3rd ed. (New York: Wiley, 1999).
6. B. Buchanan and D. Wilkins (eds.), *Readings in Knowledge Acquisition and Learning: Automating the Construction and Improvement of Expert Systems* (San Mateo, Calif.: M. Kaufmann, 1992).

CHAPTER TWELVE

MEASURING INDIVIDUAL LEARNING AND PERFORMANCE

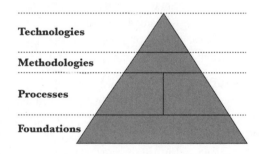

LEARNING OBJECTIVES

After reading this chapter, you will be able to do the following:

- *Discuss when* the knowledge that individuals contribute is the measure of their value to their organization.
- *Describe why* the knowledge that individuals contribute is the measure of their value to their organization.
- *Describe how* to measure the knowledge that individuals contribute to their organization.

EXPERT ADVICE

After reading this section you will be able to discuss when the knowledge that individuals contribute is the measure of their value to their organization.

Dear Mark,

I am the manager of a group of engineers. I'm always a little disappointed with our yearly performance assessment because it doesn't seem to really measure what each engineer actually did for our bottom line—or encourage them to bring more value to the company. Any ideas as to how to better assess engineering work?

Signed, "How Do We Measure the Right Things?"

Dear "How Do We Measure the Right Things,"

Years ago I worked in a group that was called on in times of crisis. One of our "stars" was famous for coming in, assessing the situation, and putting out the fire. Although he was always friendly, he never had time to teach anyone how he put out the fire—he was always on his way to another fire. At the end of the performance period, he always received a big bonus. Looking back, it's no wonder he never had time to share what he knew—that's not what he was paid for. He was paid for what he did, not for sharing what he did. And those bonuses only reinforced this truth—for him, and the rest of us.

To avoid this situation, you want to get away from the idea of focusing on what members of your group do and, instead, recognize that the knowledge they create and share is the major factor of performance. Although the other factors—motivation, resources, integrity are important to performance—it is the creation of new knowledge, and sharing that knowledge, that really increases performance for your entire group.

When it comes to assessing the performance of your engineering group, begin to focus on the knowledge that your engineers create and share. Remember, their real value to your company lies in the knowledge that they bring to bear on your company's problems—not what they do.

CONCEPT

After reading this section you will be able to describe why the knowledge that individuals contribute is the measure of their value to their organization. While you are reading this section you will learn about the following measures of individual knowledge contributions to an organization:

- Examples are a performance measure.
- Documents are a performance measure.
- Instruction is a performance measure.
- Expert advice is a performance measure.
- Performance objectives are a performance measure.
- Total knowledge assets are a performance measure.

Historically, organizations have focused on the work of their practitioners as they analyzed and applied factual and conceptual knowledge to an organizational problem and created a solution for that problem, a knowledge product. Going back to our running example using a quality plan, a quality specialist would analyze the unique requirements for a new product and apply general principles and techniques (conceptual knowledge) along with the unique factors of production (factual knowledge) to those unique requirements to create a quality plan. As discussed in Chapter Nine, this application of conceptual and factual knowledge to a specific problem results in the creation of new procedural knowledge. This creation of procedural knowledge—in this case, the embedded knowledge that resides in the quality plan—has traditionally been the measure and value of a knowledge worker. In other words, all other related activities, such as gaining access to the related factual knowledge and mastering the prerequisite conceptual knowledge, have not been seen as value-generating activities. They have not seemed to be what gets the job done. What has counted is getting a good quality plan completed. So the more organizations could minimize all other activities, such as attending training and locating and looking through process documents, the more the value-added activities—such as actually writing quality plans—could be focused on.

The focus has been only on today's production of knowledge—and that knowledge is procedural knowledge. All other types of knowledge that have been created in the development of a knowledge product—factual, conceptual, and metacognitive—have been abandoned. And often the previous knowledge product has been unavailable, making the procedural knowledge that went into that previous knowledge product unavailable for use in creating the new knowledge product. With a short-sighted focus on the knowledge needed for creating a solution for today's problem, organizations have missed the opportunity to harvest knowledge for creating a solution for tomorrow's problem. The key to measuring individual learning and performance, however, is to assess the other types of knowledge that individuals create and supply along with the current solution to today's problem. This is the knowledge that will be available for creating a new knowledge product to address tomorrow's problem—and a truer measure of the value of a worker to the organization.

Most organizations want collaboration on knowledge products. However, this results in several people working together to complete one knowledge product, making it difficult to measure individual contributions to that product. As described in Chapter Five, the work of a knowledge product can be divided by the performance objectives that have to be achieved to complete that product. Although the knowledge may be collaboratively created to achieve a performance objective through a workflow, it is typically authored initially by one individual. Although not always equivalent, the amount of knowledge created to achieve one performance is fairly comparable to the amounts of knowledge created to achieve other performance objectives. This makes the amount of knowledge created to achieve a performance objective a fairly consistent unit of measurement for individual knowledge contribution.

Examples Are a Performance Measure

When content that addresses a performance objective for a knowledge product such as a quality plan is completed, one of the first things that the author should do is to *document* the completed work as an example of work. Examples of good work provide access to procedural knowledge—the application of factual and conceptual knowledge to a specific problem. The documentation focuses on the history of the problem that the performance objective addresses. This should include the background of the larger project for the performance objective and all the major decisions and the rationales behind those decisions. For example, as mentioned in Chapter Two, a quality plan may have gone from version 1.0 to version 2.0 as a result of the design document being revised. The documentation for the performance objective content module would describe the changes in the design document and why the corresponding changes were needed in the module. The idea behind this documentation is that another quality plan specialist could easily take the example module, read the documentation, and quickly create a new module for the current quality plan.

How well a worker creates procedural knowledge and supplies it to others in the organization is one measure of his or her individual contribution to the organization. "Supplying it to others" means more than uploading the completed content module to the organization's intranet Web site. It includes documenting the content module so that its main characteristics are easily learned by other workers who may use the module as an example. And it includes tagging the module with metadata,[1] so that others can search for and find it easily. Evaluating the quality of the documentation for a content module is as important as evaluating the quality of the module itself. A well-done content module contributes to today's production. A well-done example of a content module contributes to tomorrow's production.

DOCUMENTS ARE A PERFORMANCE MEASURE

When a new content module is completed, one of the first questions for the author who created the module is, Has new factual knowledge been created during the making of this content module? Remember, factual knowledge is described as terminology, specific details, and elements. It's the type of thing we want to write down—like the steps to a process. In the case of a new content module for addressing a performance objective, were there necessary reasons not to follow the prescribed details in the current process document for creating the content module? For example, perhaps the current process document states that a summary of the marketing plan is to be placed in the content module that contains the requirements criteria for a new paper airplane. However, when the new content module was created, a better way was found to include marketing information in the module—simply place a link to the marketing report (which has an executive summary) in the module. This is a change in the process for creating the content module. Updating the process document for the content module provides a great return to the individual creating that module and to others who will later create other content modules. Authors who have created new factual knowledge during the development of their knowledge products should submit this new factual knowledge update and participate in a process to review and approve this addition to the organization's knowledge assets.

Instruction Is a Performance Measure

At the same time that factual knowledge is being reviewed after a content module is completed, another question for the author who created the module naturally follows. Has new conceptual knowledge been created during the development of this content module? Conceptual knowledge relates to theories, models, principles, and generalizations and can be broadly thought of as the general principles at work in a domain. For example, with paper airplanes, the general principles of aerodynamics are applied to create lift and the ability to steer. The principles of paper airplane design are conceptual knowledge that would go into a content module to ensure that a new airplane will perform as designed. Adding or modifying a principle of airplane design for a new and unique airplane creates new conceptual knowledge. To document this new conceptual knowledge, the associated instruction module has to be updated—because instruction is the most used method for providing access to conceptual knowledge. Typically, as discussed in Chapter Five, an organization should have a separate process for updating instruction modules.

Like the authors of new factual knowledge who must update process documents, authors who have created new conceptual knowledge in their content modules should indicate it and participate in a process to update the instructional materials accordingly. Updating conceptual knowledge should, in general, occur less frequently than updating factual knowledge does. That's because factual knowledge relates to the details of production whereas conceptual knowledge relates to the principles of production. Details will sometimes change—principles rarely change. But when they do, valuable knowledge is created that an organization can exploit the next time a content module is developed.

EXPERT ADVICE IS A PERFORMANCE MEASURE

When factual knowledge and procedural knowledge are being reviewed after a content module is completed, a final question for the author who created the module comes up. Has new metacognitive knowledge been created during the development of this content module? Metacognitive knowledge is knowledge about knowledge and involves general strategies for learning, thinking, and problem solving, including the heuristics or rules of thumb that experts use to solve problems. Expert advice is the most direct vehicle for providing access to metacognitive knowledge. Adding a new rule of thumb for creating a content module for a certain paper airplane or group of paper airplanes is the creation of new metacognitive knowledge. Just as with updating factual and procedural knowledge, a defined and separate process for accepting new expert advice should be used. Updating metacognitive knowledge should be as frequent as updating procedural knowledge. That's because metacognitive knowledge relates to when and where procedural knowledge is applied. The more unique the content modules that are created, the more expert advice is created that describes when and where those modules are most effective.

PERFORMANCE OBJECTIVES ARE A PERFORMANCE MEASURE

It turns out that providing new knowledge for a current process will only make that current process better. It will not lead to new and unique processes that fuel innovation for creating new and different products. These productivity breakthroughs are the result of what has been called *double-loop learning*—the ability of an organization to do something different and better. However, proposed changes need to be described in terms of the changes in performance they will require. Performance objectives are the key for identifying the magnitude and scope of proposed changes in the way work is done. Any significant changes in the way work is done will require the update and creation of new performance objectives. Authors who have created a new and innovative way to achieve one of the organization's larger goals that does not meet the current performance objectives should submit the needed updates and new performance objectives and participate in a process to review and approve the updated and new objectives.

Total Knowledge Assets Are a Performance Measure

How well a worker creates procedural knowledge that becomes a content module for a knowledge product has been the historical measure of that individual's contribution to the organization. However, as stated at the beginning of this section, the real key to measuring individual performance is to assess all the other types of knowledge that individuals create and supply along with the knowledge product. This is the knowledge that will be available for creating a new content module to address tomorrow's problem—and a truer measure of the real value of a worker to the organization.

Application

After reading this section you will be able to describe how to measure the knowledge that individuals contribute to their organizations. While you are reading this section you will learn about the following methods for measuring individual knowledge contributions:

- How to measure examples
- How to measure documents
- How to measure instruction
- How to measure expert advice
- How to measure performance objectives
- How to measure total knowledge assets

Historically, McBoe focused on the work of its practitioners as they analyzed and applied factual and conceptual knowledge to a McBoe problem and created a solution for that problem. For example, a quality specialist would apply general principles and techniques (conceptual knowledge) and factors of production (factual knowledge) to create the content modules of a quality plan. For McBoe, this creation of procedural knowledge—in this case the content modules of a quality plan—was the measure and value of a knowledge worker. What counted at McBoe was getting a good quality plan completed. So the more McBoe managers could minimize all other activities, such as attending training, locating and looking through process documents, and listening to war stories, the more time workers could devote to actually writing the modules for quality plans. McBoe was using only the creation of the knowledge product as the measure of individual performance. It was what workers *did* that counted for McBoe.

HOW TO MEASURE EXAMPLES

Two years ago, as mentioned in Chapter Nine, McBoe identified through a human resource (HR) survey that its experienced employees felt they were "underproducing," and follow-up interviews revealed that McBoe's experienced employees felt they were "reinventing the wheel" and were not all following "best practices" for each step in the manufacturing process. To close this perceived performance gap, McBoe instituted a best practices campaign. As also discussed earlier, McBoe sought to gather good examples, select the best ones, and post them on its intranet. It created a separate process to select the best practices; the roles in this process included submitters (authors), reviewers, and approvers. Although McBoe managers didn't know it at the time, they had started down the road to changing the way McBoe measured individual performance.

It became apparent quite soon that in order to make the campaign work, McBoe would have to make participation in the campaign part of individual performance assessment. McBoe also wanted to expand the campaign to include all the content modules that addressed the performance objectives in McBoe's knowledge products. Moreover, McBoe wanted to create each module as if it were going to be a best practice. That is, each module would be the product of a collaborative process with authoring, reviewing, and approving steps. Further, McBoe knew that if a content module was to be useful as an example, its main characteristics had to be documented, so they could be easily learned by other workers. In addition, each example module had to be easily located, so it needed to be tagged with metadata. McBoe decided to make documenting the main characteristics and tagging with metadata part of the authoring process for each content module.

TABLE 12.1.   Procedural Knowledge Contributed by an Individual.

Knowledge Products	Content Addressing Performance Objectives	Minor Revisions (× .25)	Major Revisions (× .75)	Total
Number authored (× 1.00)	40	8	4	35
Number reviewed (× .25)	20	6	2	8
Number approved (× .25)	16	6	2	7
Grand total				50

To provide some guidelines for measuring the contribution of individuals in this area, McBoe management put together a matrix for assigning a numerical value to an individual's contribution of new knowledge (that is, procedural knowledge) to content modules. Table 12.1 shows the numbers generated by an employee I'll call "Fred."

In reading Table 12.1, we see that Fred authored (created) 40 content modules to address 40 performance objectives. Out of Fred's 40 content modules, 4 had major revisions. Because another worker wrote those substantial revisions, that other worker received 0.75 of a credit per module, giving Fred only 0.25 per module and resulting in 1 credit for Fred for those 4 content modules with major revisions. Because Fred's content modules had 8 minor revisions and other workers did those minor revisions for Fred, those other workers received 0.25 of a credit per module, giving Fred 0.75 per module and resulting in 6.00 credits for Fred for the 8 modules with minor revisions. This left Fred with 35.00 credits for the content modules that he authored. Note that Fred received full credit for 28 content modules and partial credit for ones that required minor or major revisions, which gave him the total of 35 credits.

Fred also reviewed 20 content modules for others. He got 0.25 of an authoring credit for each module of content he reviewed— that gave him another 5.0 credits. He wrote 6 minor revisions and gained 0.25 of a credit for each, giving him 1.50 credits for that work. He also wrote 2 major revisions, giving him 1.50 credits. So Fred's total credits for his reviewing efforts were 8.00.

Fred also gained a 0.25 authoring credit for each of the 16 content modules that he approved, giving him 4 credits. He approved the minor revisions for 6 content modules at 0.25 of a credit each, giving him another 1.50 authoring credits. And finally, he gained another 1.50 authoring credits for approving 2 major revisions to content modules. So Fred's total here was 7.00 credits.

With everything added up, Fred received 50 credits for authoring content modules. Or said another way, because McBoe quality plans have three performance objectives, Fred contributed the equivalent of authoring nearly seventeen quality plans. This is a crude measure of his direct output of knowledge work for this time period. Note that it doesn't measure what he has learned and the other types of knowledge that he may have gained and shared during this period.

What McBoe learned from adding this assessment component to its measurement of individual performance is that *time is quality.* In other words, because McBoe doesn't deliver shabby work, it will continue to work on a plan until it meets the internal level of quality that McBoe insists on. Getting it right the first time saves time—and McBoe knows that *time is also money.* This assessment component allows individuals to see how their performance contributes to team and organizational performance.

Relate to Your Organization. Does your organization have a way to measure the procedural knowledge that an individual contributes to its content modules? Does it take into account—or give credit for—the review and approval of other workers' content modules? Does it give individuals an insight into how their contribution to the organization's procedural knowledge affects team and organizational performance?

HOW TO MEASURE DOCUMENTS

Through the same HR survey mentioned earlier, McBoe found that many newly hired employees felt poorly prepared to get their jobs done in a timely and satisfactory manner. These employees spent substantial time and effort looking up information in process documents. It also turned out that some of the information in the process documents was not up to date. This meant that new employees spent additional time and effort consulting with more experienced employees in an effort to gain the latest process information. As a result, McBoe knew it had a performance problem with updating its factual knowledge assets and making them easily accessible. To address this situation, McBoe put together a team to update the process documents and put them on the company's intranet so they were easily accessible. Problem solved—or so thought many in management at McBoe.

It wasn't long before the process documents were out of date again, and employees again spent substantial time and effort looking up information. McBoe needed an ongoing solution to this problem, one that would continually update those process documents (factual knowledge). McBoe management decided to make keeping the process documents updated part of the job of those who relied on the documents. And to make sure that people knew it was part of their job, new items were added to the assessment of individual performance.

Creating updates to a process document involves changing the process for creating a content module to include a process for collaboratively authoring the process document update, reviewing the update, and approving the update before it will be used by the others in the organization. McBoe put together a matrix for calculating an individual's contribution to the factual knowledge base of the organization. Table 12.2 displays the numbers generated for Fred by the new measures. Note that the approach is similar to calculating an individual's contribution to the content modules of an organization.

Fred authored 2 process document updates, reviewed 3 updates authored by another person, and approved 2 updates. Out of the 2 process document updates that Fred authored, one had a major revision and the other had a minor revision. Because the major revision represents substantial work that came from someone else, that person received 0.75 of a credit for the update, giving Fred only 0.25 of a credit for authoring that update. And because one of Fred's updates had a minor revision, someone else

TABLE 12.2.   FACTUAL KNOWLEDGE CONTRIBUTED BY AN INDIVIDUAL.

Factual Knowledge and Asset Creation Updates	Content Addressing Performance Objectives	Minor Revisions (× .25)	Major Revisions (× .75)	Total
Number authored (× 1.00)	2	1	1	1
Number reviewed (× .25)	3	1	0	1
Number approved (× .25)	2	1	0	0.75
Grand total				2.75

did some of the work for Fred and received 0.25 of a credit for that work, giving Fred 0.75 of a credit for his work. This left Fred with 1.00 credit for the process document updates that he authored.

Fred also reviewed 3 process document updates for others. He got 0.25 of an authoring credit for each update he reviewed, totaling another 0.75 of a credit. He wrote 1 minor revision and gained another 0.25 of a credit. He did not write a major revision. Fred's credit total for his process document update reviewing efforts was 1.00 credit.

Fred also gained 0.25 of an authoring credit for the 2 process document updates that he approved, giving him another 0.50 of a credit. He also approved a minor revision for an update, giving him an additional 0.25 of an authoring credit. Fred's credit total for his approving efforts was 0.75.

With everything added up, Fred received 2.75 credits for authoring process document updates. This again is a crude measure of his contribution to the factual knowledge base of the organization. Although the numbers are arbitrary, McBoe found them useful for getting the message to its workers that keeping the process documents updated is an important part of their jobs. It was also helpful to McBoe in broadening the scope of the responsibilities of its workers—making them aware that their job is about more than creating content modules, it also includes capturing what they learn while making those modules.

Relate to Your Organization. Does your organization have a way to measure the factual knowledge that an individual contributes to its knowledge assets? Does it take into account—or give credit for—the review and approval of other workers' knowledge assets? Does it give individuals an insight into how their contribution to the organization's factual knowledge affects team and organizational performance?

How to Measure Instruction

McBoe's HR survey also revealed that McBoe had a problem with managing its conceptual knowledge. Traditional classroom training was not bringing new hires up to speed quickly enough. As described previously, to close this performance gap, McBoe put small, refresher instruction modules on its intranet and made them accessible to employees at their desks. These small, quick modules moved employees past being stuck at the level of just trying to get what's going on and put it into memory. Again, it seemed as if the problem were solved.

As with the process documents, it wasn't long before the instruction modules were out of date. McBoe needed an ongoing solution to this problem too—one that would continually update those instruction modules. McBoe management added more new items to the assessment of individual performance. And as it had for factual knowledge, McBoe management put together a matrix for calculating an individual's contribution to the conceptual knowledge base of the organization. Table 12.3 displays the numbers generated for Fred.

Fred authored 2 instruction module updates, reviewed 1 update for another person, and approved 2 updates. As in the previous matrixes, a worker receives 1.00 credit for each instruction module that he or she authors, with a 0.25 of a credit reduction for each minor revision and a 0.75 reduction for each major revision. Workers receive 0.25 of a credit for each instruction module they review and 0.25 for each minor revision and 0.75 for each major revision that they write for a module authored by someone else. Approving instruction modules offers the same credits as reviewing does—0.25 for approving, 0.25 for each minor revision, and 0.75 for each major revision.

Table 12.3. Conceptual Knowledge Contributed by an Individual.

Conceptual Knowledge and Asset Creation Updates	Content Addressing Performance Objectives	Minor Revisions (× .25)	Major Revisions (× .75)	Total
Number authored (× 1.00)	2	1	1	1
Number reviewed (× .25)	1	0	1	1
Number approved (× .25)	2	0	0	0.5
Grand total				2.5

With everything tallied, Fred received 2.50 credits for authoring instruction module updates. McBoe knows that this too is just one crude measure of his contribution to the conceptual knowledge base of the organization. However, McBoe found these measures useful for getting the message to its workers that keeping the instruction modules updated is an important part of their jobs.

Relate to Your Organization. Does your organization have a way to measure the conceptual knowledge that an individual contributes to its knowledge assets? Does it take into account—or give credit for—the review and approval of other workers' knowledge assets? Does it give individuals an insight into how their contribution to the organization's conceptual knowledge affects team and organizational performance?

How to Measure Expert Advice

To further address the HR survey results that showed experienced employees felt they were "underproducing" and were "reinventing the wheel," McBoe sought to gather expert advice. As it had with the best practices campaign, McBoe sought to gather good advice for creating each content module, select the best pieces of advice, and post them on the McBoe intranet. And learning from the success of its best practices campaign, McBoe created a separate process to select the best advice. As before, the roles included submitters (authors), reviewers, and approvers.

It soon became apparent that as with the best practices campaign, in order to make this campaign work, McBoe would have to make participation part of the assessment of individual performance. And as with the other types of knowledge, McBoe began to realize that how well a worker creates metacognitive knowledge and supplies it as expert advice to others is one measure of individual contribution to McBoe. McBoe management put together a matrix, similar to previous assessment matrixes, for counting the contribution of metacognitive knowledge by an individual. Table 12.4 shows Fred's numbers.

Fred authored 2 expert advice modules, reviewed 2 modules for another person, and approved 2 modules. Using the same values as were used previously to measure contributions, Fred received 3.00 credits for authoring expert advice modules. Again, even though the numbers are arbitrary, McBoe found them useful for getting the message to its workers that providing expert advice is an important part of their job and contributes to the bigger picture of the company's knowledge base.

Relate to Your Organization. Does your organization have a way to measure the metacognitive knowledge that an individual

TABLE 12.4. METACOGNITIVE KNOWLEDGE CONTRIBUTED BY AN INDIVIDUAL.

Metacognitive Knowledge Asset Creation and Updates	Content Addressing Performance Objectives	Minor Revisions (× .25)	Major Revisions (× .75)	Total
Number authored (× 1.00)	2	1	1	1.00
Number reviewed (× .25)	2	0	1	1.25
Number approved (× .25)	2	1	0	0.75
Grand total				3.00

contributes to its knowledge assets? Does it take into account—or give credit for—the review and approval of other workers' knowledge assets? Does it give individuals an insight into how their contribution to the organization's metacognitive knowledge affects team and organizational performance?

How to Measure Performance Objectives

McBoe management thought that it had covered all the knowledge types that an individual could contribute to his or her team and company. However, after the managers took a step back and really looked at the additions they had made to individual assessment, it seemed that something wasn't quite right. As one manager reflected, "If we continually update our process documents, instruction, and expert advice, we will continually improve the way we currently do things. But with so much attention to improving the way we currently do things, we will miss the opportunity to do something different and much better." They didn't know it at the time, but they were recognizing the difference between single-loop learning—getting better at what one is currently doing—and double-loop learning, doing something different and better (discussed in Chapter Thirteen). McBoe managers recognized that the underlying performance objectives of work define what the organization currently does. They then quickly realized that performance objectives can also describe what the organization might do instead—something different and better. Real changes that usher in real organizational improvements will mean changing the underlying performance objectives of work. In the same way that it had for the other ways that individuals contribute knowledge and gain credit, McBoe put together a matrix for counting the contribution of updating current performance objectives and creating new ones. Table 12.5 displays Fred's contribution.

Fred authored 1 new or updated performance objective. McBoe managers didn't want to give more credit for creating a new performance objective than for modifying an existing one. Their reasoning was that they didn't want to provide an incentive for generating new performance objectives when they might not be needed. Table 12.5 also shows that Fred reviewed 2 performance objectives and approved 1 objective. Adding it all up as before,

TABLE 12.5. PERFORMANCE OBJECTIVE UPDATES CONTRIBUTED BY AN INDIVIDUAL.

Performance Objectives Creation and Updates	Content Addressing Performance Objectives	Minor Revisions (× .25)	Major Revisions (× .75)	Total
Number authored (× 1.00)	1	1	0	0.75
Number reviewed (× .25)	2	1	0	0.75
Number approved (× .25)	1	0	0	0.25
Grand total				1.75

Fred received 1.75 credits for authoring performance objectives. Now McBoe had in place a way to reward people for thinking about what McBoe might do—something different and better—instead of thinking only about the current way of doing things.

Relate to Your Organization. Does your organization have a means to reward people for coming up with a way to do things differently and better? Does it have a way to map new ways of doing things into performance objectives? Does it take into account—or give credit for—the review and approval of other workers' proposed updates and new performance objectives? Does it give individuals an insight into how their contribution to the performance objectives underlying their work affects team and organizational performance?

How to Measure Total Knowledge Assets

Once an individual's contribution to the different types of knowledge was known, McBoe thought that individual employees could also benefit from knowing how much total knowledge they contributed to the knowledge assets of the company during a performance period. Table 12.6 shows the totals for Fred's contribution to knowledge products, performance objectives, and knowledge assets for McBoe (that is, the totals for Tables 12.1, 12.2, 12.3,

Table 12.6. Total Knowledge Contributed by an Individual.

Individual Knowledge Products and Assets	Fred
Procedural Knowledge	50
Factual Knowledge	2.75
Conceptual Knowledge	2.5
Metacognitive Knowledge	3
Performance Objectives	1.75
Total Knowledge Products	50
Total Knowledge Assets and Performance Objectives	10
Total Contribution: Products, Assets, and Objectives	60
Assets and Objectives to Products Ratio	20%

and 12.4). It also illustrates the knowledge that Fred has contributed over and above his creation of content modules for knowledge products (Table 12.1).

Note that Fred contributed 50 modules of content to knowledge products and 10 modules of content to knowledge assets and performance objectives for a total contribution of 60 modules. That works out to 20 percent of his work and accomplishments being attributed to creating and updating knowledge assets and performance objectives. Interviews with workers like Fred revealed that it did take more effort on the part of workers to document these modifications to knowledge assets and performance objectives, however, it was actually much less than 20 percent more work. The reason being that workers were creating this new knowledge in their work before; they were just not documenting it. Workers estimated that the new documentation processes added around 10 percent more work for them. As shown in the next chapters, this additional 10 percent in work will contribute greatly to individual, team, and organizational learning and provide the opportunity for innovation that leads to improved organizational performance.

Relate to Your Organization. Does your organization have a way to measure the total knowledge that an individual contributes to its knowledge assets and performance objectives? Does it take into account—or give credit for—the review and approval of other workers' knowledge assets or performance objectives? Does it give individuals an insight into how their total contribution to the organization's knowledge assets affects team and organizational performance?

Note

1. *Tagging with metadata* means adding key words to a document so that it can be easily found by a computer search.

CHAPTER THIRTEEN

IMPROVING TEAM LEARNING AND PERFORMANCE

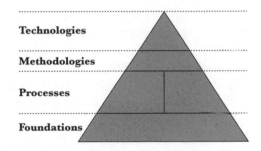

LEARNING OBJECTIVES

After reading this chapter you will be able to do the following:

- *Discuss when* team learning is more than the sum of individual learning.
- *Describe why* team learning is more than the sum of individual learning.
- *Describe how* to improve team learning in your organization.

EXPERT ADVICE

After reading this section you will be able to discuss when team learning is more than the sum of individual learning.

Dear Mark,

Our organization would like to take a more "team-oriented" approach in assessing the performance of individuals. In other words, we want to reward people on the overall success of their team, not by their individual accomplishments. Can you give us some help on this?

Signed, "Playing a Team Game"

Dear "Playing a Team Game,"

When I was in the seventh grade, I learned from my basketball coach, Mr. Overlund, how to focus on team performance rather than on my own accomplishments. In one of the first games of the season, I remember getting a rebound and dribbling the ball the length of the court to score a basket for our team. After I did this a second time, the coach replaced me with another player and had me sit next to him on the bench while he explained the value of the *assist* in team performance. An assist in basketball is when you pass the ball to another player on your team who makes a basket. The coach explained that providing an assist was as good as scoring a basket because it resulted in a basket for the team. He wanted me to change my focus from the points that I scored for myself to the points that the team scored.

Your organization needs to start keeping statistics around the assists that team members provide that contribute to the overall performance of your teams. Assists come in several forms, such as contributing to process documents and instructional modules, creating good work examples, and providing expert advice. Remember, just like players on sports teams, your team members need to know which activities contribute to team output in your organization.

CONCEPT

After reading this section you will be able to describe why team learning is more than the sum of individual learning. While you are reading this section you will learn about the following approaches to improving learning in groups:

- Single-loop learning
- Double-loop learning
- Team learning

SINGLE-LOOP LEARNING

Single-loop learning is the way most people approach a problem. It is learning the best-known method for solving the problem. (See Argyris and Schön's *Organizational Learning II,* for a detailed account of single-loop and double-loop learning.[1]) Novices will know little about the problem and the possible solutions. They require access to conceptual knowledge in order to understand the problem and formulate a solution. Therefore novices are seeking instruction as a way to learn how to solve the problem. Practitioners have solved similar problems before—they require access to procedural knowledge. They are seeking an example that they can learn from and can adapt as a solution to the current problem. Experts may not know immediately how to solve the problem, but they can quickly assess what kind of problem it is and what solutions may work. Experts have metacognitive knowledge— knowledge about knowledge—and can provide access to it in the form of expert advice for novices and practitioners to use in learning how to apply the best-known method for solving the problem. Improving single-loop learning at the team level means decreasing the time it takes the team to bring the best-known solution to a current problem. Direct access to appropriate knowledge assets and to people with tacit knowledge of the problem is required for teams to decrease the time to the best-known solution.

In examining team performance, one of the first questions that should be asked is, Does this team have access to the latest factual knowledge that relates to its work? If the answer is no, then the question becomes, How can we make the latest factual knowledge available to this team? Will it mean adding a new team member who has access to this factual knowledge in tacit form? This new team member could then provide the latest factual knowledge through the tacit-explicit-tacit cycle, beginning with telling it to the other team members. Or will it mean providing newly created factual knowledge in an explicit form and giving the team access to updated documents. Providing the knowledge to the team in a tacit form has been labeled the *personification approach*. Providing it to the team in an explicit form has been labeled the *codification approach*. In either case, if the team does not have access to the latest factual knowledge—and lack of that knowledge is inhibiting team performance—then providing this access will, obviously, improve team performance. Because in most organizations most factual knowledge should be made explicit and accessible, most "fixes" for a shortfall of factual knowledge employ the codification approach, making factual knowledge available in a document as soon as it is updated.

In examining team performance, one of the next questions that should be asked is, Does this team have access to the latest conceptual knowledge that relates to its work? If the answer is no, then the question becomes, How can we make the latest conceptual knowledge available to this team? Will it mean taking a personification approach and adding a new team member who has this new conceptual knowledge in tacit form and who can provide on-the-job instruction to team members? Or will it mean taking a codification approach and providing this conceptual knowledge in an explicit form, giving the team access to newly updated instruction modules? The choice for your team will not be as clear-cut as in the case of factual knowledge. If your larger organization is moving toward a codification approach for all instruction, then probably the best approach for your team is a codification one. However, if your larger organization hasn't invested in codifying the conceptual knowledge needed for the work of your team, then a personalization approach may make more sense in the short run. That is, bring in a new team member who can do on-the-job training for the other team members. In either case, if the team does not have access to the latest conceptual knowledge—and lack of that knowledge is inhibiting team performance—then providing access to this knowledge will, obviously, improve team performance.

Yet another question that should be asked in considering team performance is, Does this team have access to the procedural knowledge that directly relates to its work? If the answer is no, then the question becomes, How can we make procedural knowledge that directly relates to its work available to this team? Will it mean taking a personification approach by adding a new team member who has access to directly related procedural knowledge in tacit form and who can provide an example of a solution for a problem closely related to the one the team is working on? Or will it mean taking a codification approach by providing the procedural knowledge that directly relates to the team's work in an explicit form and giving the team access to a documented example of a solution? The choice for your team will be easier than in the previous case concerning conceptual knowledge. If your larger organization is moving toward a codification approach for best practices, then maybe the best approach for your team is a codification one. However, if your larger organization hasn't invested in codifying best practices, then a personalization approach may be your only choice. That is, bring in a new team member who can provide a relevant example of a solution for the other team members. However, in the long run the best approach will probably be a mix of the codification and personalization approaches. Access to a relevant example augmented with personal communication with the expert who provided the example will provide the team members with access to all the missing procedural knowledge (tacit and explicit) they need for performance improvement.

The final question that should be asked when examining team performance is, Does this team have access to the metacognitive knowledge it needs to successfully complete its work? If the answer is no, the question becomes, How can we make the relevant metacognitive knowledge available to this team? Will it mean taking a personification or a codification approach to provide the needed metacognitive knowledge for the team? As discussed in Chapter Eight, because metacognitive knowledge is mostly tacit in organizations, you will have to pursue a personalization approach. That is, you will need to bring in a new team member (perhaps, on a temporary basis) to provide the needed expert advice. If your larger organization is moving toward a codification approach for capturing some of the gems of expert advice, then you may be able to leverage some decision support capabilities by codifying expert advice. However, as with examples of good work, you will probably need to augment the decision support capability with personal communication with the expert who supplied the advice in order to provide team members with access to all the missing metacognitive knowledge (tacit and explicit) they will need for performance improvement.

DOUBLE-LOOP LEARNING

Double-loop learning is an innovative way to solve a problem. Typically, it involves employing a different way of seeing a problem. It's the application of a new principle or a unique way of applying a known principle to a problem. The result of double-loop learning is a fundamental change in the way work is accomplished. The change in performance objectives for the workers dictates the magnitude and scope of change in the way work is done. After the performance objectives are updated, then related factual, conceptual, procedural, and metacognitive knowledge needs to be updated to reflect this change in accomplishing work. That means that new materials for the related process document, instruction module, example, and expert advice are created for the new and updated performance objectives—replacing the old materials that described how to accomplish the work in the old way. Innovation at the team level begins with all team members having access to the different types of knowledge—factual, conceptual, procedural, and metacognitive—so that the current best way of solving a problem is known to all members of the team. Knowing what they know, the team members are now prepared to look at innovative ways to solve the current problem. This is where the best thinking of the past meets the best thinking of the present to create the best solutions for tomorrow. Innovation requires a team to build off what it knows—otherwise the team will invent the same solutions over and over again.

TEAM LEARNING

If your team is low on access to the latest conceptual, procedural, or metacognitive knowledge, a team manager may use a personalization approach and add a worker to the team for the express purpose of providing access to that knowledge. A team can begin going down this path by taking a hard look at its current members and identifying the types of knowledge that are not easily accessible by any member. Then the search becomes one of finding an individual who has the needed knowledge and will share it with the team. That individual's contribution to the knowledge of the team can boost the total knowledge created by the team beyond just that individual's contribution.

Application

After reading this section you will be able to describe how to improve team learning and performance in your organization. While you are reading this section you will learn how to improve team learning and performance in three ways:

- How to support single-loop learning
- How to support double-loop learning
- How to support team learning

How to Support Single-Loop Learning

Table 13.1 shows the individual contributions of knowledge to the Quality Plan team as measured at the end of a performance period. As presented and discussed in Chapter Twelve, Fred's

Table 13.1.   Individual Contributions of Knowledge
to the Quality Plan Team.

Team Knowledge Products & Assets	Fred	John	Betty	Bob	Total
Performance Objectives	1.75	0.5	0.25	0.25	2.75
Factual Knowledge	2.75	1	1	1	5.75
Conceptual Knowledge	2.5	1	1	1	5.5
Procedural Knowledge	50	48.5	34	31	163.5
Metacognitive Knowledge	3	0	0	0	3
Total Knowledge Products	50	48.5	34	31	163.5
Total Knowledge Assets and Performance Objectives	10	2.5	2.25	2.25	17
Total Contribution: Products, Assets, and Objectives	60	51	36.25	33.25	180.5
Assets and Objectives to Products Ratio	20%	5%	7%	7%	10%

contribution was 50 for knowledge products—that means he authored content modules that addressed 50 performance objectives for a knowledge product. Because quality plans have three performance objectives, that's the equivalent of authoring nearly seventeen quality plans. Fred also contributed some of the knowledge that he gained through his work in the form of factual knowledge (process document updates), conceptual knowledge (instructional updates), and metacognitive knowledge (expert advice) for an additional 10 credits for authoring a knowledge product. This gives Fred a grand total of 60 authoring credits—the equivalent of authoring 20 quality plans. Fred's numbers show that he is an experienced, efficient, and motivated worker. John has almost as much experience as Fred. John gets almost as much work done on knowledge products as Fred, however, it is Fred that provides the lion's share of knowledge assets and updates to performance objectives for this team. Betty and Bob are new hires and their numbers show it. They are contributing about half what Fred does to the knowledge products of the team. Consequently, John, Betty, and Bob are all lagging behind Fred in contributing to knowledge assets and performance objectives with numbers well below 10 percent of their total effort while Fred contributes 20 percent of his total effort to the modification of assets and objectives.

Knowing that novices need access to factual knowledge is one of the reasons that McBoe made the changes that made more explicit factual knowledge available to employees than before, a difference displayed in the contrast between Figures 8.1 and 8.2. To make its factual knowledge more explicit and accessible, McBoe shortened its cycle time for updating its manuals, thereby reducing the amount of tacit factual knowledge that was undocumented at any given time. This gave McBoe's teams greater access to the latest factual knowledge and allowed modest improvements in team performance, given that team members spent less time ensuring that the team was working off the latest factual knowledge. In the quality plan team, this meant that Betty and Bob had access to the latest process documents updated by Fred—reducing their time spent accessing factual knowledge.

As also represented in the differences between Figures 8.1 and 8.2, McBoe worked to make most of its conceptual knowledge explicit and to provide access to it through instruction. McBoe had instructional designers work with subject matter experts to write small instruction modules for each performance objective and put them on the company intranet along with the manuals. Because McBoe was moving toward a codification approach for all instruction, it was decided that the quality plan team members would leverage this investment by using the modules, but it was also decided that the team members would have a connection to one of the experts who had provided the module content. This expert provided some subtle insights (tacit knowledge) that the team members used to augment the online modules. The end result was greater team performance because Betty and Bob had access to the latest instruction modules made by Fred, and they also knew they could follow up with this more experienced worker if they had questions.

McBoe also worked to make much of its procedural knowledge explicit (Figures 8.1 and 8.2) and to provide access to this knowledge through examples. Then, to make it easy for McBoe employees to gain access to those examples, McBoe put them on its company intranet along with the manuals and instruction modules. Because McBoe had already begun taking steps to address this situation with a codification approach (documenting examples of work), it was decided to augment each documented example with a link to the worker who had created it. For Betty and Bob, access to a relevant documented example and personal communication with the creator of the example provided them with access to all the missing procedural knowledge (tacit and explicit) they needed for performance improvement. Finally, McBoe made more of its metacognitive knowledge explicit (Figures 8.1 and 8.2) and provided access to it through expert advice. To make it easy for McBoe employees to gain access to these pieces of advice, McBoe put them on the company intranet. However, the quality plan team manager knew that metacognitive knowledge remains mostly tacit in organizations and that the team would therefore also have to pursue a personalization approach. It was decided to bring in a new team member to provide the needed expert advice. Moreover, to make the most of this new expert, he or she was to leverage the organization-wide codification initiative for capturing gems of expert advice as a decision support capability. As with examples of good work, the quality plan team manager felt the team needed to augment the decision support capability with personal communication with the expert who had supplied the expertise. This provided team members with access to all the missing metacognitive knowledge (tacit and explicit) they needed for performance improvement.

Relate to Your Organization. Does your team spend too much time ensuring that it is working off the latest factual knowledge? Does your team have access to both the explicit and tacit forms of the conceptual, procedural, and metacognitive knowledge it needs to do its work?

How to Support Double-Loop Learning

Two years ago McBoe's quality plan development team knew it had a problem with its quality plans. It was found that the quality plans were not being used by the testing report team when it created evaluations of products. Upon follow-up questioning by McBoe's process improvement team, the testing report team members confided that they felt they had to rewrite the requirements criteria of the quality plans in order to develop effective measures of performance for the products. This revealed a situation where a different way of solving the problem was needed—that is, a different way of creating quality plans and testing reports that would ensure the quality that McBoe wanted in its paper airplane products.

McBoe knew that the answer to changing the way it created quality plans and testing reports lay in changing the underlying performance objectives for the quality plans and testing reports. The process improvement team, along with the quality plan development team and the testing report team, went through an exercise where they reviewed Performance Objective 3 for quality plans and Performance Objective 6 for testing reports. They found that although these performance objectives were very similar, they were also different. And it was evident they were different enough to be interpreted and addressed differently by both teams—causing a mismatch between the two groups as they were creating requirements criteria for McBoe products.

When the process improvement team, along with the quality plan development and testing report teams, considered

Performance Objective 3 and Performance Objective 6, they saw the similar wording and found that the underlying intent was the same for both performance objectives. However, they also saw the possibility for different interpretations by the quality plan and testing report teams. These two teams finally settled on writing one performance objective that met the intent of both. (See Chapter Eighteen for a detailed account of this update of performance objectives and the associated knowledge assets.)

As a result of this exercise to combine and update performance objectives, McBoe had experienced double-loop learning. For the quality plan team and the testing report team, a new and different way of seeing the problem had been adopted. It resulted in a fundamental change in the way work was accomplished. The change in performance objectives for the teams in this example dictated the magnitude and scope of change in the way work was done. After the new performance objective was created and the objectives it replaced were deleted, the related process document, instruction module, example, and expert advice were created for the new performance objective. Because the quality plan development team and the testing report team both knew how they currently did their work, they were prepared to look at innovative ways to solve their current problem. Performance objectives were then a *common language* that the teams used to come to agreement on a new way of working. At the team level, this is how McBoe used the best thinking of the past and combined it with the best thinking of the present to create the best solution for tomorrow.

Relate to Your Organization. Does your team really know how it does its work? Does your team know the underlying performance objectives of its work? Can your team use the best thinking of the past and combine it with the best thinking of the present to create the best solution for tomorrow?

How to Support Team Learning

The McBoe manager of the quality plan team was still concerned about the team's low productivity. In order to respond to a greater demand for McBoe products, this manager knew that this team would need to produce more—about fifty percent more! She had already increased current productivity with updated performance objectives and the addition of more explicit knowledge assets, as discussed earlier. (And Betty and Bob were doing much better than had previous employees with their level of experience.) Now the team manager was looking at hiring more people— probably two more. Then an intriguing thought struck her. Let's look at the knowledge the team is generating and see if we can improve it with hiring the *right* person. Looking at the numbers for Fred, John, Betty, and Bob (Table 13.1), the manager noticed that these existing team members were creating a high number of new content modules for knowledge products but were quite low in generating new knowledge assets. This manager knew the implications of this situation. It meant that the team was getting the work done—but not learning new ways to do it better and differently in the future. She thought, "Let's bring in someone who will help us create more knowledge assets and boost innovation to build better future products."

Table 13.2 shows the individual contributions of knowledge to the quality plan team after Alice joined it. And as Table 13.2 illustrates, Alice was the answer to the problem of helping the quality plan team create more knowledge assets and boost innovation. Alice's numbers show that she is a team player. Although she doesn't outshine anyone in the creation of knowledge products, she does shine in contributing to the other knowledge assets and performance objectives. And look what she does for the productivity of the other team members! Although John's overall output improved slightly, Fred's improved quite a bit, and Betty and Bob really increased their productivity. Alice's contribution to the explicit knowledge assets was one obvious thing that improved their productivity. However, there was also the less obvious effect of the addition of Alice's tacit knowledge assets. In other words, Alice did her work, including contributing to the explicit knowledge assets. However, she also provided Betty and Bob with access to her vast level of tacit knowledge. More simply put, she shared with them what she knew. And look what her influence did for Betty and Bob in their contributions to knowledge assets and performance objectives (compare Tables 13.1 and 13.2). Betty's numbers increased from 7 percent to 10 percent and Bob's numbers

TABLE 13.2. ADDING A WORKER TO IMPROVE TEAM PERFORMANCE.

Team Knowledge Products & Assets	Fred	John	Betty	Bob	Alice	Total
Performance Objectives	1.75	0.5	0.25	0.25	2.75	5.5
Factual Knowledge	2.75	1.25	2	2	3	11
Conceptual Knowledge	2.5	1.5	2	1.5	3	10.5
Procedural Knowledge	54.5	49.25	44.25	41	42.5	231.5
Metacognitive Knowledge	3.5	0	0	0	5.25	8.75
Total Knowledge Products	54.5	49.25	44.25	41	42.5	231.5
Total Knowledge Assets and Performance Objectives	10.5	3.25	4.25	3.75	14	35.75
Total Contribution: Products, Assets, and Objectives	65	52.5	48.5	44.75	56.5	267.25
Assets and Objectives to Products Ratio	19%	7%	10%	9%	33%	15%

increased from 7 percent to 9 percent. Both are not currently as high as Fred's but their contributions are going in the right direction. Alice was just the right person to add to this team to make it more productive—from a personality point of view and from a knowledge point of view. She improved the team by much more than her individual contribution.

Relate to Your Organization. Is your team underproducing? Does it have access to all the knowledge it needs to get high-quality work done in a timely way? Is your team learning new ways to do the work better and differently in the future? Would the addition of the *right* new team member bring the right knowledge to the team and add greatly to its productivity?

Note
1. C. Argyris and D. Schön, *Organizational Learning II: Theory, Method, and Practice* (Reading, Mass.: Addison Wesley, 1996).

CHAPTER FOURTEEN

MANAGING ORGANIZATIONAL LEARNING AND PERFORMANCE

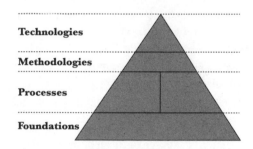

LEARNING OBJECTIVES

After reading this chapter you will be able to do the following:

- *Discuss when* organizational learning is more than the sum of team learning.
- *Describe why* organizational learning is more than the sum of team learning.
- *Describe how* to improve your organizational learning.

EXPERT ADVICE

After reading this section you will be able to discuss when organizational learning is more than the sum of team learning.

Dear Mark,

I am the manager of a group of knowledge workers. Our company is look-ing at how we can do more knowledge work and do it better. We have all heard that we need to work "smarter," not harder, but realistically, how do we go about doing that? Where do we start with something like this?

Signed, "How Do We Get Smarter?"

Dear "How Do We Get Smarter,"

Where I live, we had the wettest summer on record this past summer. Like a lot of other homeowners, my wife and I found that we had a leak in our roof. I went up on the roof with the roof repair expert and estimator. After a quick gaze, he said, "Here's your problem; the flashing wasn't installed property when the house was built." I never told him that I'd been on that roof several times and couldn't locate the leak. He then gave me an estimate that I accepted immediately. After all, I knew what I was paying for—the expert knowledge that he used to find the leak. I would also be paying for a young roofer to reinstall the flashing. These two people gave me better service than either would have by himself. The young roofer probably wouldn't have found the leak, and the old expert hasn't practiced his roofing skills for some time.

As a manager of knowledge workers, you want them to see that the *whole* of the knowledge they can bring to your company's problems will need to be greater than the *sum of its parts.* Begin by focusing on the knowledge products these workers produce, and identify the knowledge that goes into those products. Ask, who provides it? What knowledge can be added that will improve the products and deliver them faster? Remember, you want to instill a vision for collaborative work and innovative learning in your organization—that's the way for your company to begin to work smarter, not harder.

CONCEPT

After reading this section you will be able to describe why organi-zational learning is more than the sum of team learning. While you are reading this section you will learn about the following methods for improving organizational learning:

- Single-loop learning
- Double-loop learning
- Organizational learning

SINGLE-LOOP LEARNING

To improve organizational performance, you must first understand where your starting point is. That involves identifying your knowledge products, how they are created, and the knowledge assets available at the organizational level during their creation. For each knowledge product that is identified, the level of collaboration should be assessed. Levels of collaboration can be *informal, defined,* or *unknown.* Each knowledge product should also be assessed in terms of the level of definition of the performance objectives for that product. Level of definition can be *unknown, partially complete,* or *complete.* Additionally, each knowledge product should be assessed to determine whether the knowledge assets needed for supporting workers in meeting that product's performance objectives are easily accessible. Knowledge assets can be listed for each knowledge product to give an idea of the level of support that they provide to learners for achieving the product's performance objectives.

An organization can then go on to define its collaboration processes, identify a complete set of performance objectives for the knowledge products, and create a full set of knowledge assets for each product, with links to the subject matter experts responsible for the content of those assets. This sets the stage for single-loop learning at the organizational level. Now the organization not only knows what knowledge assets it has, but it can now track the flow of knowledge used to create those assets. Using tracking data to improve the flow of knowledge results in decreasing the time it takes to bring the best-known solutions to the problems faced by the organization.

DOUBLE-LOOP LEARNING

Double-loop learning is the same for organizations as it is for teams; it is the creation of an innovative way to solve a problem. Although it's the application of a new principle or a unique way of applying a known principle to a problem, at the organizational level it typically means that this new principle or way of application cuts across organizational boundaries. And as with double-loop learning in teams, performance objectives are the key to double-loop learning in organizations. Performance objectives not only show what work is to be done and how that work will be judged, but also show how work is interconnected within an organization. This interdependency between performance objectives allows *systemic* learning and organizational performance improvements. An example of systemic learning (introduced in Chapter Thirteen and presented in detail in Chapter Eighteen) is the situation in which the same performance objective is addressed in the creation of two separate knowledge products. A change in this performance objective then affects the creation of both knowledge products. Knowing this allows management to consider the organizational, or systemic, view of the impact of any proposed change before it is approved and instituted. If this systemic view were lacking, the performance objective might be changed for one of the knowledge products and any broader impacts, possibly negative ones, involving other products might not be known until sometime later. The ability to track the consequences of changes across the work of an organization has been termed *systems thinking*. (An often-quoted reference for systems thinking is Senge's *The Fifth Discipline*.[1]) Without systems thinking, organizations find themselves continually taking two steps forward and one back as they institute changes—some with positive consequences and some with negative ones—to improve organizational performance. In many organizations the negative consequences cancel out the positive ones, resulting in little, if any, actual performance improvement. Using performance objectives to institute changes across an organization reduces the opportunity for these negative consequences to occur and leads to more systemic organizational performance improvements.

ORGANIZATIONAL LEARNING

As with a team, if an organization is low on access to the latest conceptual, procedural, or metacognitive knowledge, a strategy should be formulated for the express purpose of providing access to that knowledge. The goal should be to provide access to the knowledge needed to create all the knowledge products across the organization. However, facilitating organizational learning is more than making sure that the teams for each knowledge product have access to the knowledge they need. It is ensuring that collaborative processes exist that allow teams to change the performance objectives for their work. These processes also allow teams to change shared performance objectives, ones addressed in two or more knowledge products by different teams. By improving these *interconnected* performance objectives and updating associated knowledge assets, a team's contribution to the knowledge of the organization can boost the total knowledge created by the organization beyond just that team's contribution.

Application

After reading this section you will be able to describe how to improve your organizational learning. While you are reading this section you will learn how to support learning in organizations in three ways:

- How to support single-loop learning
- How to support double-loop learning
- How to support organizational learning

How to Support Single-Loop Learning

Table 14.1 shows the results of a quick analysis of how well the McBoe Company was supporting single-loop learning before it took the idea of iLearning to heart. In this simplified example, McBoe's four knowledge products—design document, quality plan, testing report, and user document—are evaluated in terms of level of collaboration, level of definition of their performance objectives, and accessibility of needed knowledge assets. The collaboration process for the design document has been identified as *informal,* meaning that there seems to be a process but it is not always followed in the same way. The performance objectives for the design document are *unknown,* meaning no objectives for the creation of a design document are known to have been defined. Finally, only *incomplete instruction* is available for those involved in

TABLE 14.1. STARTING POINT FOR THE McBOE COMPANY.

Knowledge Product	Collaboration Process	Performance Objectives	Knowledge Assets
Design document	Informal	Unknown	Incomplete instruction
Quality plan	Defined	Complete	All present, link to subject matter experts
Testing report	Defined	Complete	Instruction, examples
User document	Unknown	Unknown	None

collaboratively creating a design document. Perhaps this instruction is all that remains from some design document training course in the past. In contrast, the quality plan has a defined collaboration process, a complete set of performance objectives, and a full set of knowledge assets has not only been developed but is easily accessible and has links to the subject matter experts responsible for asset content. The testing report has a defined collaboration process and a complete set of performance objectives but lacks a complete set of knowledge assets, having only some instruction modules and examples available. And finally, the user document has no defined collaboration process, no known performance objectives, and no known knowledge assets for those involved in creating a user document. It makes one wonder how the team ever gets a user document done. At the time of this initial assessment, the McBoe Company was creating around twenty-five unique paper airplane products per year.

It took McBoe a year to identify its knowledge products, define the collaboration processes, identify a complete set of performance objectives for the knowledge products, and create a full set of knowledge assets for each product with links to the subject matter experts responsible for the content of those assets. Table 14.2 shows McBoe's support of single-loop learning one year after it completed this initial phase of iLearning at the organizational level. (Note that at this time, McBoe was creating the quality plan as part of the design document, so there are no data for the quality plan alone.) Now McBoe not only knew what knowledge

Table 14.2. The Flow of Knowledge at the McBoe Company.

Team Knowledge Products & Assets	Design Document	Testing Report	User Document	Total
Performance Objectives	6	3	2.5	11.5
Factual Knowledge	13	8	6	27
Conceptual Knowledge	12	9.5	7.5	29
Procedural Knowledge	500	250	250	1000
Metacognitive Knowledge	7	6.25	5.25	18.5
Total Knowledge Products	500	250	250	1000
Total Knowledge Assets and Performance Objectives	38	26.75	21.25	86
Total Contribution: Products, Assets, and Objectives	538	276.75	271.25	1086
Assets and Objectives to Products Ratio	8%	11%	9%	9%

assets it had in a *static* sense, it also had a feeling for the *flow* of knowledge in the company. That is, McBoe could see how many instances of the different types of knowledge were being created during a performance period.

Reading the first column of Table 14.2, which looks at the flow of knowledge around the design document, we see that the first row shows that 6 performance objectives were created or updated. As with the knowledge assets, creating or updating performance objectives is a team effort, with a process that includes authoring, reviewing, and approving. The Factual Knowledge row reveals that the team creating design documents contributed 13 updates to process documents modules that provided access to factual knowledge. The Conceptual Knowledge row shows that the design document team contributed content for 12 instruction modules that provided access to conceptual knowledge. The Procedural Knowledge row shows that the design document team was responsible for creating 500 design document content modules. Each content module was also documented so it could serve as an example, thereby providing access to the procedural knowledge that went into the design documents. Finally, the design document team contributed content for 7 expert advice modules that provided access to metacognitive knowledge. The team's total work on design documents during this year resulted in creating or updating 538 modules for design documents, knowledge assets, and performance objectives. The design document team contributed 38 modules to knowledge assets and performance objectives, that means 8 percent of the team's work and accomplishments can be attributed to creating and updating knowledge assets and performance objectives. However, that is still below the target amount of 20 percent for an iLearning organization.

During this year, McBoe created content modules to address a thousand performance objectives in the design and building of new paper airplanes. Given twenty-eight performance objectives for all knowledge products in McBoe's design and build manufacturing process, that corresponds to creating thirty-five new unique airplanes per year. Even with all the overhead of collaboratively creating knowledge assets, that's a 40 percent increase in productivity when compared with the twenty-five unique products put out two years before.

At the time when McBoe was creating the quality plan as part of the design document, management felt McBoe was losing some of its commitment to quality during the development of the design document. However, before McBoe committed to iLearning, decisions about resolving this problem were driven only by hunches about what might work. The data shown in Table 14.2 quickly made it evident that the design document process was bloated in comparison with processes for the other knowledge products. It was obvious that cognition was not evenly distributed in knowledge products across the manufacturing process and that quality plans were not effective knowledge producers as part of the design document; this indicated that McBoe had, in effect, a hole in this process where reasoning leaked out. Making the quality plan a separate knowledge product with its own process plugged that hole and more evenly distributed cognition across the McBoe manufacturing process. Table 14.3 shows the results of this more even distribution of cognition. Note that after breaking out the quality plan from the design document, workers on quality

TABLE 14.3. THE QUALITY PLAN AS A SEPARATE KNOWLEDGE PRODUCT.

Team Knowledge Products & Assets	Design Document	Quality Plan	Testing Report	User Document	Total
Performance Objectives	3.25	2.75	3	2.5	11.5
Factual Knowledge	6.75	6.25	8	6	27
Conceptual Knowledge	6	6	9.5	7.5	29
Procedural Knowledge	336.5	163.5	250	250	1000
Metacognitive Knowledge	4	3	6.25	5.25	18.5
Total Knowledge Products	336.5	163.5	250	250	1000
Total Knowledge Assets and Performance Objectives	20	18	26.75	21.25	86
Total Contribution: Products, Assets, and Objectives	356.5	181.5	276.75	271.25	1086
Assets and Objectives to Products Ratio	6%	11%	11%	9%	9%

plans only contributed 6 percent of their total effort to creating and updating knowledge assets and performance objectives. This low contribution indicates that breaking out the quality plan was a good decision because it wasn't getting the attention previously that it should have.

Relate to Your Organization. Does your organization know whether cognition is evenly distributed in its knowledge products across its processes? Does any knowledge product appear bloated when compared to the other knowledge products? Is there a hole where reasoning is leaking out?

How to Support Double-Loop Learning

McBoe's management team also knew that the company had a strategic problem with its quality plans. However, by breaking the quality plan out as a separate knowledge product and focusing at the team level on improving quality plans, McBoe was able to begin a process of double-loop learning. As discussed in the previous chapter, on team learning and performance, McBoe's process improvement team found that quality plans were not being used by the testing report team to create performance evaluations of products. Even though the quality plan development team and testing report team addressed similar performance objectives, these objectives were different enough to create a mismatch between the two groups in creating requirements criteria for McBoe products. The result was duplication of work and more iteration of review and approval cycles in the evaluation of McBoe products.

Table 14.4 shows the results of updating the performance objectives for the quality plan development team and the testing report team. After the new performance objective was created and the two objectives it replaced were deleted, the related process document, instruction module, example, and expert advice were created for the new performance objective. This profoundly reduced duplication of work and iterations of review and approval for evaluation of McBoe products. Note the increase in the content created for quality plans and testing reports during the following year (compare Tables 14.3 and 14.4). Updates on performance objectives increased from 2.75 to 7.00 for quality plans and 3.00 to 6.00 for testing reports. Factual knowledge updates increased from 6.25 to 15.00 for quality plans and from 8.00 to 10.00 for testing reports. Conceptual knowledge updates increased from 6.00 to 14.50 for quality plans and from 9.50 to 11.25 for testing reports. Procedural knowledge updates—where the work gets done—increased from 163.5 to 243.5 for quality plans and from 250 to 270 for testing

Table 14.4. McBoe's Double-Loop Learning at the Company Level.

Team Knowledge Products & Assets	Design Document	Quality Plan	Testing Report	User Document	Total
Performance Objectives	7	7	6	2.5	22.5
Factual Knowledge	14.25	15	10	6	45.25
Conceptual Knowledge	13	14.5	11.25	7.5	46.25
Procedural Knowledge	336.5	243.5	270	250	1100
Metacognitive Knowledge	10	11.25	8.25	5.25	34.75
Total Knowledge Products	336.5	243.5	270	250	1100
Total Knowledge Assets and Performance Objectives	44.25	47.75	35.5	21.25	148.75
Total Contribution: Products, Assets, and Objectives	380.75	291.25	305.5	271.25	1248.75
Assets and Objectives to Products Ratio	13%	20%	13%	9%	14%

reports. And finally, metacognitive knowledge updates increased from 3 to 11.25 for quality plans and from 6.25 to 8.25 for testing reports.

During this year, McBoe created content modules to address 1248.75 performance objectives in the design and building of new paper airplanes. Again, given twenty-seven performance objectives (remember that two were combined into one) for all knowledge products in McBoe's design and build manufacturing process, that corresponds to creating forty-six new unique airplanes over this year. That's almost a 33 percent increase in productivity over the year before. This tremendous increase in productivity is a result of the knowledge product teams' dramatic increase in their contributions to the knowledge assets and performance objectives of their processes. Although not all teams are contributing at the 20 percent level McBoe is well on its way to becoming an iLearning organization.

Relate to Your Organization. Does your organization have a means to gather measures of knowledge contribution at the team level so management can provide direction strategically from the organizational level?

How to Support Organizational Learning

McBoe could not have realized the single-loop learning effects described earlier without having done the work to create and support its collaborative workflows for developing knowledge products, managing performance objectives, and creating and updating knowledge assets. Those workflows were the means for ensuring that teams had access to knowledge needed to effectively create all the knowledge products across the company. They were also the means for updating the performance objectives for the quality plan development team and the testing report team— resulting in double-loop learning at the organizational level. Finally, McBoe used learning and performance data collected at the individual level, consolidated at the team level, and aggregated at the organizational level to provide a picture of the flow of knowledge across the company. McBoe used this picture to direct its process improvement efforts at the organizational level. In this way, McBoe used the best thinking of the past and combined it with the best thinking of the present to create a better McBoe for the future.

Relate to Your Organization. Does your organization have collaborative workflows for developing knowledge products, managing performance objectives, and creating and updating knowledge assets? Does it have learning and performance data at the organizational level to provide a picture of the flow of knowledge across the organization?

Note

1. P. Senge, *The Fifth Discipline: The Art and Practice of the Learning Organization* (New York: Doubleday/Currency, 1990).

PART FOUR

APPLYING METHODOLOGIES AND DEPLOYING TECHNOLOGIES

CHAPTER FIFTEEN

REUSING KNOWLEDGE ASSETS

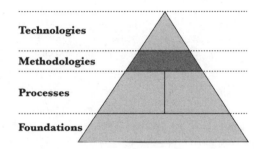

Technologies

Methodologies

Processes

Foundations

LEARNING OBJECTIVES

After reading this chapter you will be able to do the following:

- *Discuss when* to employ reusable learning objects for developing knowledge assets.
- *Discuss why* to employ reusable learning objects for developing knowledge assets.
- *Describe how* to employ performance objectives in order to reuse knowledge assets as learning objects in your organization.

EXPERT ADVICE

After reading this section you will be able to discuss when to employ reusable learning objects for developing knowledge assets.

Dear Mark,

I've recently taken a new position as a training manager at a large government agency. Although I have managed groups before, this is my first time managing a training group. Since I have taken the position, I have heard a lot about building training materials out of "reusable learning objects." Could you explain what they are and the benefits of using them?

Signed, "Learning the Ropes"

Dear "Learning the Ropes,"

Reusable learning objects are based on a concept that comes from the field of software engineering. In developing software you begin by identifying all the places in the overall system where code will be needed to perform a similar function. Then, instead of developing many copies of this code and distributing them across the system, a good practice is to put the code in a module and have the system execute that module each time that function is needed. The benefit is that if the function needs changing, that change can be made in only one place (the module) and still be in effect across the whole system. This approach reduces errors and costs due to updates.

Reusable learning objects embody an effort to use this same approach in developing instructional content. In the reusable learning object approach, instead of developing many copies of the same content that will appear in many places in a large lesson or course of study, that content is placed in a single module, and that module can then be referenced when that content is needed as part of the lesson or course of study.

Remember, it takes more work to build courses with reusable learning objects. As with software engineering, you have to take a look to see if the benefits of improving quality and reducing costs for updates are worth the extra time and money. As you might guess, for larger projects the benefits usually are worth it, but for smaller efforts this approach doesn't pay off.

Concept

After reading this section you will be able to describe why to employ reusable learning objects for developing knowledge assets.

While you are reading this section you will learn about the following aspects of knowledge assets:

- Knowledge assets can be organized into learning objects.
- Knowledge assets can be reused.

KNOWLEDGE ASSETS CAN BE ORGANIZED INTO LEARNING OBJECTS

The two performance objectives that are part of the process outlined in Figure 15.1 were originally described differently but were later found to be fundamentally the same. Performance Objective 2 (addressing product life expectancy) for a quality plan is really the same as Performance Objective 4 (addressing durability) for a testing report. Figure 15.1 also shows why performance objectives can be used to organize the content of a learning object. For example, if a user were in the process of creating a quality plan and accessed Performance Objective 2, he or she would have access to all the knowledge assets associated with that performance objective—expert advice, an example, an instruction module, and the process document that describes what needs to be done. Together, these knowledge assets make up a learning object that provides access to all four types of knowledge—factual, conceptual, procedural, and metacognitive. Each of the knowledge assets can also be thought

FIGURE 15.1.   KNOWLEDGE ASSETS ORGANIZED INTO LEARNING OBJECTS.

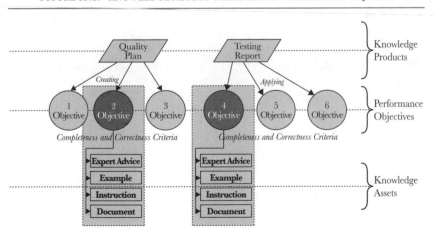

of as an information object—one that provides access to one of the four types of knowledge. Similarly, if a user were in the process of creating a testing report and accessed Performance Objective 4, the user would have access to all the knowledge assets associated with that performance objective, giving the user access to the knowledge assets needed to achieve that performance objective. Because Performance Objectives 2 and 4 are fundamentally the same, the assets associated with them can be the same.

Knowledge Assets Can Be Reused

Finding that performance objectives are fundamentally the same creates an opportunity for reusing knowledge assets as learning objects. As in the previous example, the same set of knowledge assets, organized as a learning object, could be associated with Performance Objective 2 (addressing product life expectancy) for a quality plan and Performance Objective 4 (addressing durability) for a testing report. Because these two performance objectives when treated as a single learning object would share a set of knowledge assets, updating any asset for one performance objective would update it for the other performance objective as well. That makes reuse of knowledge assets simple and easy to track. (For helpful information on using performance objectives to organize instructional content into learning objects, see Barritt and Alderman's *Creating a Reusable Learning Objects Strategy*.[1])

Application

After reading this section you will be able to describe how to employ performance objectives in order to reuse knowledge assets as learning objects in your organization. While you are reading this section you will learn about the following techniques:

- How to organize knowledge assets
- How to reuse knowledge assets

How to Organize Knowledge Assets

At the McBoe Company it was no coincidence that a performance objective for addressing product life expectancy for a quality plan was almost identical to another performance objective addressing durability for a testing report. When McBoe put together the teams to write the performance objectives, it put the same people on the team that wrote the quality plan objectives and on the team that wrote the testing report objectives. Even with the same members on both teams they wrote very similar yet slightly different versions of what was essentially the same performance objective. Here's what they originally wrote for Performance Objective 2 (addressing product life expectancy) for a quality plan:

> State the requirements, criteria, and conditions for the product life of the airplane.

And here's what the same team wrote for Performance Objective 4 (addressing durability) for a testing report:

> State the requirements, criteria, and conditions for the durability of the airplane.

After these performance objectives were written, knowledge assets were created for workers to achieve those objectives. A process document, an instruction module, an example, and some expert advice were developed for each performance objective, creating a learning object for that objective.

Relate to Your Organization. Has your organization established a process improvement process that reviews the underlying performance objectives for each knowledge product in its business process? Does it use those performance objectives to organize knowledge assets to help workers achieve those objectives?

How to Reuse Knowledge Assets

In its process improvement activity, McBoe decided to go through its entire business process and list all the performance objectives for each step that had to be addressed. During this exercise the performance objectives deemed unnecessary were to be dropped. This didn't turn out to be a big deal because only a few were found to be unnecessary. (These few existed because changes in the process had been made without updating the associated performance objectives.) Afterward, the process improvement team was to combine all performance objectives that were essentially the same. By combining similar performance objectives and eliminating redundant ones, McBoe was also trying to reduce the number of total performance objectives.

When the process improvement team considered quality plan Performance Objective 2 and testing report Performance Objective 4, they saw the similar wording and found that the underlying intent was the same for both performance objectives. They then went about the business of writing one performance objective that met the intent of both. Here is the result of their effort.

State the requirements, criteria, and conditions for the life expectancy of the airplane.

Using the process improvement process depicted in Figure 5.4, the McBoe process improvement team sent the proposed change to reviewers representing the detailed design process and the implementation process. After review the proposed change was approved and became the official way to do business at McBoe.

As a result, McBoe had one performance objective that met the needs of the two objectives that it had replaced. And McBoe could list one fewer performance objective for its paper airplane manufacturing process. More important, McBoe could now combine the two sets of knowledge assets into one set to support workers in achieving the new performance objective. Now the workers addressing product life expectancy for a quality plan and the workers addressing durability for a testing report are looking at the same performance objective and the same knowledge assets when it comes to measures of life expectancy and the level of life expectancy for the airplane. As a company, McBoe knows a little more about how it does its work and is in a better position to do something different that cuts across the company.

Relate to Your Organization. Has your organization uncovered similar performance objectives that are addressed in different knowledge products of its business process? Has it come up with a process for combining similar performance objectives and reusing them?

Note
1. C. Barritt and F. Alderman, *Creating a Reusable Learning Objects Strategy: Leveraging Information and Learning in a Knowledge Economy* (San Francisco: Pfeiffer, 2004).

CHAPTER SIXTEEN

REPURPOSING KNOWLEDGE ASSETS

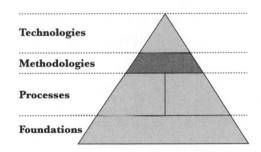

Technologies

Methodologies

Processes

Foundations

LEARNING OBJECTIVES

After reading this chapter, you will be able to do the following:

- *Discuss when* to employ repurposed knowledge assets instead of reusable knowledge assets.
- *Describe why* repurposed knowledge assets are different from reusable knowledge assets.
- *Describe how* to employ performance objectives in order to identify and repurpose knowledge assets in your organization.

EXPERT ADVICE

After reading this section you will be able to discuss when to employ repurposed knowledge assets instead of reusable knowledge assets.

Dear Mark,

I have heard the term "reuse" solutions and I have heard the term "repurpose" solutions. Are they the same? If they aren't—what's the difference?

Signed, "The Same But Different"

Dear "The Same But Different,"

I once heard a story about a guy in college who "reused" his girlfriend's paper for a class that he was taking. She had written the paper for a similar class that she was taking at another institution. At first he was quite proud of his own cleverness in avoiding all the work of actually writing a paper for his class. However, as things sometimes go (and restore our faith in the fairness of our world), his professor gave him extensive feedback for rewriting the paper so that it would meet the performance objectives of the class. Not happy with all this extra work but unwilling to admit his dishonesty, he set himself to the task of "repurposing" his earlier submission. As you might guess, this review and revise cycle went through several iterations. In the end, he was not guilty of cheating himself out of the opportunity to improve himself through an educational experience. He did not "reuse" his girlfriend's paper. And he did not "repurpose" her paper either, because his final product held no resemblance to his first (borrowed) submission.

Remember, the same lesson is true for our work in an organizational setting. We *reuse* solutions when we don't change them in any way. We *repurpose* solutions when we modify them and use them in another context. However, the important point—one that the subject of this story learned so well—is that sometimes it is better to create solutions from scratch than to try to modify a solution that will not translate to another context.

CONCEPT

After reading this section you will be able to describe why repurposed knowledge assets are different from reusable knowledge assets. While you are reading this section you will learn about these two concepts of knowledge assets:

- Knowledge assets can be shared.
- Knowledge assets can be repurposed.

KNOWLEDGE ASSETS CAN BE SHARED

Figure 16.1 shows two performance objectives that are almost the same: Performance Objective 3 addressing flight maneuvers and distance in a quality plan, and Performance Objective 6 addressing flight length and acrobatics in a testing report. If a user accessed either performance objective, he or she would see all the knowledge assets associated with it—expert advice, an example, an instruction module, and the process document that describes what needs to be done. Even though Performance Objectives 3 and 6 are very similar and the process documents that describe them have a lot in common, they also have some details that are different. Because of these objectives' similarities, workers can apply the same general principles and techniques to satisfy them. As the shading in Figure 16.1 illustrates, the instruction module for both performance objectives can be the same. This situation forms a basis for *repurposing* knowledge assets. However, because not all knowledge assets can be shared between Performance Objectives 3 and 6, each will need its own versions of the assets that cannot be shared. So Performance Objective 3 and Performance Objective 6 share a subset of knowledge assets, and in addition, each possesses a unique set of knowledge assets that describes the *context* in which the performance objective is achieved.

FIGURE 16.1.   KNOWLEDGE ASSETS CAN BE SHARED.

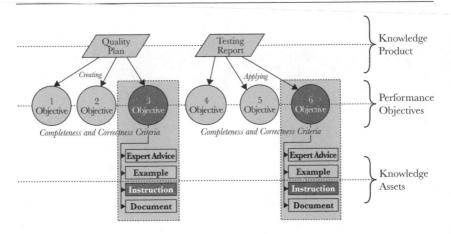

KNOWLEDGE ASSETS CAN BE REPURPOSED

Figure 16.2 depicts another situation in which knowledge assets are partly shared. However, this situation is more complicated in that each of the similar performance objectives may be interpreted differently by different parts of the organization. For example, two physical sites may write quality plans and they may address Performance Objective 3 differently. Site A may achieve it in a slightly different way than Site B does. Site A may follow Performance Objective 3 very literally, and Site B may follow a slightly different interpretation of that objective (the one labeled Objective 7 in Figure 16.2).

Again, if the site differences in interpreting Performance Objective 3 are very small, workers can apply the same general principles and techniques to satisfy Performance Objective 3 at both sites. This means that the instruction module for both sites can be the same, but the other knowledge assets must be different. So the same instruction module can be used for Sites A and B; however, there are two versions of the process document, the example, and the expert advice—one for Site A and one for Site B. Again, this creates a situation of sharing some knowledge assets but not all of them. Each site needs its own set of unique knowledge

FIGURE 16.2. KNOWLEDGE ASSETS CAN BE REPURPOSED.

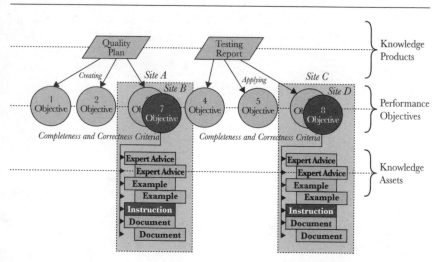

assets to describe the *context* in which the performance objective is addressed. This is true for the testing report written at Sites C and D too. These sites share the same instruction module, but need different process documents, examples, and expert advice to achieve their slightly different performance objectives. (See my article for a detailed and referenced discussion on using performance objectives to reuse and repurpose knowledge work.[1])

APPLICATION

After reading this section you will be able to describe how to employ performance objectives in order to identify and repurpose knowledge assets in your organization. While you are reading this section you will learn these techniques:

- How to share knowledge assets
- How to repurpose knowledge assets

HOW TO SHARE KNOWLEDGE ASSETS

When the process improvement team at McBoe reviewed Performance Objectives 3 and 6, they went through an exercise similar to the one they had completed when they reviewed Performance Objectives 2 and 4, as described in Chapter Fifteen. Again, even with the same team members reviewing both performance objectives, the team wrote very similar yet slightly different versions of what was essentially the same performance objective. Here's what it originally wrote for Performance Objective 3, addressing flight maneuvers and distance for a quality plan.

> State the requirements, criteria, and conditions for airplane flight maneuvers and distance.

And here's what the same team wrote for Performance Objective 6, addressing flight length and acrobatics for a testing report.

> State the requirements, criteria, and conditions for testing the flight length and acrobatics of the airplane.

Again, the process improvement team's aim was to combine all performance objectives that were essentially the same. And as in the reuse example in Chapter Fifteen, McBoe was also trying to reduce the total number of performance objectives by combining similar objectives and eliminating redundant ones.

When the process improvement team considered Performance Objective 3 and Performance Objective 6 together, team members saw the similar wording and found that the underlying intent was the same for both objectives. They then went about the business of writing one performance objective that met the intent of both. Here is the result of their effort:

State the requirements, criteria, and conditions for the flight distance and acrobatic maneuvers of the airplane.

However, unlike the quick and happy ending a new objective produced in the reuse example described in Chapter Fifteen, an underlying problem remained with the new wording suggested for this objective. Engineers developing the quality plan wanted to put in wording stating that the testing conditions would be consistent with the delivery environment. That is, the paper airplane would be tested in a way that would predict how well it would fly for the customer that bought it. The engineers wanted to know whether the paper airplane held up to its quality plan. The manufacturing managers wanted to put in wording stating that the conditions would be consistent with the manufacturing environment. During McBoe's manufacturing process the airplane paper is dampened so it will mold more easily during the final assembly process. If you try to fly the airplane immediately after assembly, it will fly only about half as far as it will later when it is dry. The manufacturing managers wanted to adjust the expectations so everyone, including those preparing the testing report, would know that they were doing their job well—soggy planes just don't fly very far.

After much discussion, it became apparent that most of the performance objective was the same at both places in the process (the quality plan and the testing report) and that the instruction could be the same for both places in the process, but that some adjustment was needed due to the way the performance objective was temporarily affected in the manufacturing process. An obvious option would be to have two performance objectives—one for the quality plan and one for the testing report. However, this option would not meet the company goal of reducing total performance objectives by combining similar objectives and eliminating redundant ones. So the team went back to the drawing board and came up with a solution.

Relate to Your Organization. Has your organization established a process improvement process that reviews the underlying performance objectives for each knowledge product in its business process? If it has, is there a way to identify performance objectives that are very similar even though not exactly the same?

HOW TO REPURPOSE KNOWLEDGE ASSETS

McBoe's solution was to combine the performance objectives into one performance objective. A user in the process of creating a quality plan who accesses the document that described Performance Objective 3 and a user in the process of creating a testing report who clicks on the document that described Performance Objective 6 now see documents that have almost the same text. The initial text they see is identical and describes the common aspect of Performance Objectives 3 and 6, reading as follows:

> State the requirements, criteria, and conditions for the flight distance and acrobatic maneuvers of the airplane.

However, if the user is creating a quality plan under Performance Objective 3, he or she then sees the following additional text in the document, stating the additional conditions necessary for a quality plan:

> Requirements criteria are to be measured in respect to the customer's delivery environment.

And if the user is creating a testing report under Performance Objective 6, he or she sees the following additional text in the document, stating the additional conditions necessary for a testing report:

> Requirements criteria are to be measured at the manufacturing site.

Because the McBoe process improvement team members knew that Performance Objectives 3 and 6 were very similar, they determined that the same general principles and techniques could be applied to satisfy them. This meant that the instruction module for both performance objectives could be the same. However, because addressing this performance objective involves a slightly different process at both places in the manufacturing process, a single complete set of knowledge assets could not be used to address the performance objective. Moreover, additional text would be needed in each of the two process documents to describe the specific application of the final performance objective to the appropriate knowledge product: the quality plan or the testing report.

This was not the end of the story for McBoe's first effort at sharing knowledge assets. This same process improvement team soon discovered that McBoe's workers applied this performance objective a little differently not only in the quality plan and testing report but also at the different sites that did the same work. Another engineering group, Site B, when writing a quality plan always described the conditions for performance in respect to its own testing facility, situated at an altitude of 9,000 feet. Because Site A focused on the conditions that its customers experienced, it was in line with Site B only when a customer wanted a paper airplane delivered to an address at 9,000 feet. Similarly, Site D, another manufacturing facility, was concerned about the time of day that performance was measured. Site C always measured at the beginning of the next day, so its airplanes were damp but not soggy. Site D measured right after assembly, because it was running three shifts and had no room for inventory. Consequently, Site D wanted a big reduction in the expected length of flight because its planes were always quite soggy.

The process improvement team, to its credit, worked through all the implications of these differences (without any fistfights) and came up with the following description of the performance objectives to be addressed at the two different sites.

The common description read:

> State the requirements, criteria, and conditions for the flight distance and acrobatic maneuvers of the airplane.

The quality plan description for Site A went on to state:

Requirements criteria are to be measured in respect to the customer's delivery altitude.

The quality plan description for Site B went on to state:

Requirements criteria are to be measured at 9,000 feet above sea level.

The testing report description for Site C went on to state:

Requirements criteria are to be measured at the manufacturing site. Measures will be taken at least 12 hours after final assembly.

And finally, the testing report description for Site D went on to state:

Requirements criteria are to be measured at the manufacturing site. Measures will be taken within 4 hours after final assembly.

By again revisiting Performance Objectives 3 and 6, the team had determined that they were, indeed, very similar. So the team agreed that workers apply the same general principles and techniques to satisfy them—regardless of the knowledge product or site. This meant that the instruction module for both performance objectives could be left the same. However, although much of the text in the process document was applicable to all the knowledge products and manufacturing sites, there was to be additional and separate text for Sites A, B, C, and D that described how the performance objective would be met for the different product conditions and at the different sites. The identical text was on the first page of the document, and the knowledge product and site-specific text was on the second page. Attentive readers will note the foreshadowing in this decision. Later, we will read how McBoe broke these pages apart so that management of the shared knowledge assets could be automated.

Relate to Your Organization. Does your organization have performance objectives that are addressed uniquely in different business process products? How about objectives that are addressed uniquely at different sites of your organization? And finally, has your organization come up with a process for combining similar performance objectives and repurposing their knowledge assets?

Note

1. M. Salisbury, "A Framework for Reusing and Repurposing Knowledge Work in Organizations," *Journal of Information and Knowledge Management,* 7(2), Sept. 2008, 1–11.

CHAPTER SEVENTEEN

ORGANIZING
KNOWLEDGE ASSETS

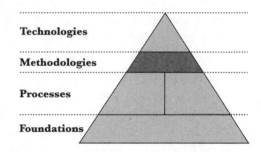

LEARNING OBJECTIVES

After reading this chapter you will be able to do the following:

- *Discuss when* to organize knowledge assets in organizations.
- *Describe why* it's important to organize knowledge assets in organizations.
- *Describe how* to organize knowledge assets in your organization.

EXPERT ADVICE

After reading this section you will be able to discuss when to organize knowledge assets in organizations.

Dear Mark,

In our organization, when one of the regulations changes for our industry, we spend a lot of time and effort in updating our manuals,

instructional materials, and examples of work. In fact, it seems that
we are spending more time on these supporting materials than
on our "real work." Any suggestions for helping us turn this around?

Signed, "Swamped by Updates"

Dear "Swamped by Updates,"

Years ago when I was growing up, my mom wrote the phone numbers of friends and relatives in the back of our phone book. Afterward, the rest of us started writing the phone numbers of our friends in the back of that book. This worked fine until we got a new book. Then we would start writing the numbers of new friends and the changed numbers of old friends in the back of the current phone book. As a result, we had a stack of old phone books that contained our "family database" of phone numbers. Updating a phone number in that stack didn't mean it was updated everywhere else it might be listed in that stack.

Your organization could benefit greatly from unifying all its supporting materials in a way that will make it easier to make updates when changes in regulations occur. By *unifying,* I mean that for every regulation, you describe how to address that regulation with as generic a description as possible. Then at every appropriate place in your supporting materials, you make a placeholder for that generic description.

Remember, unlike the situation with my family's stack of phone books, once you have unified materials, when there is a change in a regulation, you can go to a single place in your supporting materials, make an update, and that update is automatically made everywhere that regulation is addressed in your materials.

CONCEPT

After reading this section you will be able to describe why it's important to organize knowledge assets in organizations. While you are reading this section you will learn about the following benefits of linking knowledge assets:

- Knowledge assets can be linked for reuse.
- Knowledge assets can be linked for repurposing.

KNOWLEDGE ASSETS CAN BE LINKED FOR REUSE

Figure 17.1 shows shared knowledge assets falling naturally into a linked network of assets. When users have to address Performance Objective 2 & 4, they all have access to the same set of knowledge assets—whether they are addressing the performance objective for a quality plan or a testing report or addressing this objective at different sites. (The & signals that two performance objectives have been combined into one objective.) This way, whenever the knowledge assets for this combined performance objective are changed, they will be changed for all users, no matter which knowledge product they are working on (quality plan or testing report) or which site they are working at.

KNOWLEDGE ASSETS CAN BE LINKED FOR REPURPOSING

As outlined in Figure 17.2, because Performance Objectives 3, 6, 7, and 8 are very similar, workers will apply the same general principles and techniques to satisfy them. That means that a shared, or *common*, process document that describes what needs to be done can be used for all four performance objectives. This is also true for common instruction that describes why things need to be done and some common expert advice that describes how to do it. This process document, instruction, and expert advice are

FIGURE 17.1. KNOWLEDGE ASSETS CAN BE LINKED FOR REUSE.

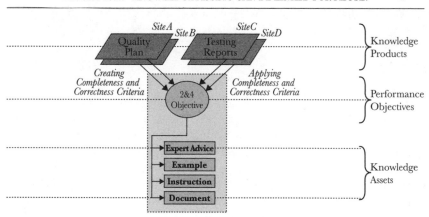

FIGURE 17.2. KNOWLEDGE ASSETS CAN BE LINKED FOR REPURPOSING.

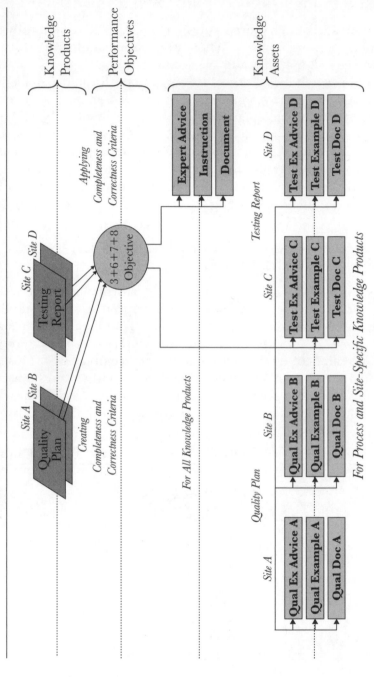

shared knowledge assets. However, not all knowledge assets are shared between the four performance objectives. Each performance objective has its own unique set of knowledge assets that describe the *context* (place in the process or physical site) in which the performance objective is addressed. For example, Figure 17.2 shows a shared process document, instruction, and expert advice whether Performance Objective 3 + 6 + 7 + 8 is accessed by a worker writing a quality plan at Site A or Site B or by a worker writing a testing report at Site C or Site D. (The + signals that the four performance objectives share common knowledge assets but that each has additional knowledge assets not shared with the others.) However, depending on what part of the process they are completing (quality plan or testing report) or what site they are working at, workers will access additional and different contextual knowledge assets. For instance, a worker at Site A who is writing a quality plan would access a process document, an example, and expert advice specifically tailored for Site A. Similarly, a Site B worker writing a quality plan would access the same types of materials but specifically tailored for Site B, a Site C worker writing a testing report would access materials for Site C, and a Site D worker writing a testing report would access materials for Site D.

Figure 17.2 shows how shared knowledge assets are linked in such a way that they can be accessed from many places— different sites and different places in the business process. Note that only part of the performance objectives for writing a quality plan and writing a testing report are shown. Imagine how much more complexity there is even in this simple example that is not shown.

Application

After reading this section you will be able to describe how to organize knowledge assets in your organization. While you are reading this section you will learn the following techniques:

- How to link knowledge assets for reuse
- How to link knowledge assets for repurposing

How to Link Knowledge Assets for Reuse

McBoe found that to share knowledge assets was a simple and rather straightforward task. As Figure 17.1 shows, it was simply a matter of mapping their intranet site so that when users clicked on Performance Objective 2 & 4 they were taken to the same set of knowledge assets—regardless of what they worked on in the process (quality plan or testing report) or what site they worked at. Whenever the knowledge assets for this combined performance objective were changed, they were changed for all workers.

Relate to Your Organization. Are you facing a straightforward situation where workers in your organization can easily share knowledge assets over an intranet? Can you easily connect performance objectives to knowledge assets, knowledge products, and the business process of your organization?

How to Link Knowledge Assets for Repurposing

McBoe wanted to implement a strategy in which the company would share knowledge assets—assets tied to the manufacturing process. However, as Figure 17.2 shows, when some but not all knowledge assets are shared between performance objectives, things get a bit messier for any organization. At first, McBoe tried the same manual approach it used for sharing reusable knowledge assets, as described earlier. This approach started to fall apart when McBoe considered that depending on what knowledge product users were working on (quality plan or testing report) or what site they were working at, they should see a different set of knowledge assets.

How to manage such complexity was the problem that McBoe faced. Clearly, it couldn't just start implementing this strategy and hope to get it right and avoid constructing a quagmire. No, it obviously needed some systematic way to go about building and documenting what it built. So, beginning at the beginning, McBoe developers created a table to show how knowledge products fit into the larger process picture. That is, they created a table that showed the main processes, subprocesses, knowledge products,

Table 17.1. McBoe's Processes, Subprocesses, Knowledge
Products, and Performance Objectives.

Main Process	Subprocess	Knowledge Product	Performance Objective
Design	Detailed	Quality plan	3678
Build	Implement	Testing report	3678

and performance objectives of the McBoe manufacturing process. Table 17.1 is a simplified version of their table.

Reading the first row of Table 17.1, from left to right, reveals that the design main process has a subprocess (the design detailed), which has a knowledge product (quality plan), with a performance objective (3678). Because Table 17.1 is a simplification of McBoe's manufacturing process, it shows only one knowledge product for each subprocess and only one subprocess for each main process. Note that Performance Objective 3678 is addressed in both the quality plan and testing report knowledge products.

Next, McBoe developers created a table to show how performance objectives are related to sites and how they both are related to knowledge assets. Reading the first row of Table 17.2 from left to right, we read that Performance Objective 3678 for all sites has knowledge assets Document 3678, Instruction 3678, and Expert Advice 3678. Document 3678 contains the actual description of Performance Objective 3678. It also contains the process details for achieving Performance Objective 3678. The second row of Table 17.2 shows the contextual knowledge assets for addressing Performance Objective 3678 at Site A. These knowledge assets are Qual Doc 3678A, Qual Example 3678A, and Qual Ex Advice 3678A. Qual Doc 3678A contains the text that has been amended to the common description of Performance Objective 3678. And it contains the process details for achieving Performance Objective 3678 at Site A. Table 17.2 also shows the contextual knowledge assets for addressing Performance Objective 3678 at Sites B, C, and D.

It was a lot of work, but McBoe developers had documented how their main processes were broken down into subprocesses, knowledge products, and performance objectives for those

TABLE 17.2. McBOE's PERFORMANCE OBJECTIVES, SITES, AND KNOWLEDGE ASSETS.

Performance Objective	Site	Process Document	Instruction Module	Example	Expert Advice
3678	All	Document 3678	Instruction 3678		Expert Advice 3678
3678	A	Qual Doc 3678A		Qual Example 3678A	Qual Ex Advice 3678A
3678	B	Qual Doc 3678B		Qual Example 3678B	Qual Ex Advice 3678B
3678	C	Test Doc 3678C		Test Example 3678C	Test Ex Advice 3678C
3678	D	Test Doc 3678D		Test Example 3678D	Test Ex Advice 3678D

products. Next, they associated the performance objectives with the knowledge assets needed to address them at the specific company sites. This documentation would allow them to quickly update their knowledge assets and avoid mistakes while doing it. Again, attentive readers will note the foreshadowing in this work. Later, we will read how McBoe used these tables to update its knowledge assets.

Relate to Your Organization. Is your organization facing the same complexity problems as the McBoe Company faced in repurposing knowledge assets? Has it documented how its main processes are broken down into subprocesses, knowledge products, and performance objectives for those products? Does it have a systematic way to associate performance objectives with the knowledge assets needed to address those objectives in specific situations?

CHAPTER EIGHTEEN

MANAGING KNOWLEDGE ASSETS

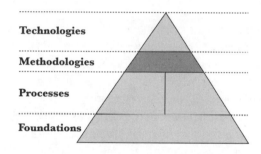

LEARNING OBJECTIVES

After reading this chapter you will be able to do the following:

- *Discuss when* to systematically update reused and repurposed knowledge assets.
- *Describe why* it's important to systematically update reused and repurposed knowledge assets.
- *Describe how* to systematically update reused and repurposed knowledge assets in your organization.

EXPERT ADVICE

After reading this section you will be able to discuss when to systematically update reused and repurposed knowledge assets.

Dear Mark,

I'm the manager of a group that makes training materials for our corporation. Most of our materials have been used in a traditional classroom setting. Now, we have been given a new corporate initiative that tasks us with also providing the same materials in a Web-based format and making them available on a just-in-time basis so that they can be accessed from a PDA. We are buried now just with the work for keeping our training materials current. Any ideas on how we can keep all these formats up to date without losing our minds?

Signed, "Update Fever"

Dear "Update Fever,"

Your group has to develop a systematic approach for updating your training materials. I recommend using the underlying performance objectives of work as the basis of that systematic approach. These underlying performance objectives of work are the "criteria" or "guidelines" for what constitutes successful completion of the work. Sometimes they are spelled out as regulations that have to be addressed or technical issues that have to be solved. If you can identify the underlying performance objectives of work, then you can associate your training materials with those performance objectives. Afterward, when a performance objective of training has changed, all you have to do is systematically follow up on all the training materials that are associated with that performance objective and update them.

Remember, even though a computer database is the ideal tool for this sort of thing, you could create a systematic approach to updating your materials by using a metal filing cabinet and folders as tools. The main idea is to first make sure that each performance objective includes a complete list of the materials associated with that objective. Then, when a performance objective is changed, you can use that list to find all the materials that need to be updated.

CONCEPT

After reading this section you will be able to describe why it's important to systematically update reused and repurposed knowledge assets. While you are reading this section you will learn about the following aspects of updating knowledge assets:

- Knowledge assets can be reused.
- Knowledge assets can be repurposed.

KNOWLEDGE ASSETS CAN BE REUSED

The main advantage of reusing knowledge assets is that updating becomes straightforward. For example, updating Performance Objective 2 & 4 (Figure 18.1) is just a matter of the process improvement team getting agreement from representatives of the workers who create quality plans in the detailed step (at Sites A and B) and from representatives of the workers who create testing reports in the implementation step (at Sites C and D). Once an updated description is agreed on by all these representatives of the workers who will be affected by the proposed change, then it is simply a matter of making the appropriate revisions in the knowledge assets that address Performance Objective 2 & 4. Once all the

FIGURE 18.1. KNOWLEDGE ASSETS CAN BE REUSED.

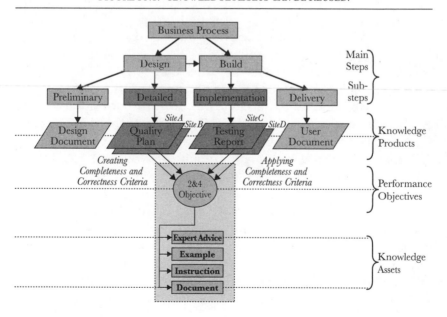

materials are revised, it doesn't matter which step in the process (detailed or implementation) workers are completing or which site (A, B, C, or D) they are working at, the knowledge assets will be the same.

Knowledge Assets Can Be Repurposed

Similarly, the main advantage of repurposing knowledge assets is making automatic updates of knowledge assets possible. In Figure 18.2 for example, updating repurposed knowledge assets begins by revising the common process document that describes what needs to be done for all four combined performance objectives $(3 + 6 + 7 + 8)$. As Figure 18.2 illustrates, if these revisions affect other knowledge assets held in common, such as the instruction module and expert advice, then these other assets would also be updated.

Updating repurposed knowledge assets becomes more complicated, however, when the performance objectives for different knowledge products or at different sites are affected by a unique product or site context. Revising the common process document may affect what workers do in creating quality plans and testing reports. It may also affect the workers differently at the various sites. For example, as outlined in Figure 18.2, a worker at Site A writing a quality plan may have to do things quite differently after the document that describes the common elements is changed. That means that the document describing the performance objective—Qual Doc A (quality plan document for Site A)—will need to be updated too. And the two other knowledge assets associated with the contextual performance objective for a quality plan at Site A—Qual Ex Advice A and Qual Example A (expert advice and example for quality plan at Site A)—will also have to be updated. However, the worker at Site B trying to write a quality plan may go unaffected by the change in the common process document, so Qual Doc B and the associated knowledge assets (expert advice and example) may not need to be updated. Similarly, a worker at Site C trying to write a testing report may have to do things quite differently after the changes, but a worker at Site D trying to write a testing report may go unaffected. So, Test Doc C and its associated knowledge assets would need to

Figure 18.2. Knowledge Assets Can Be Repurposed.

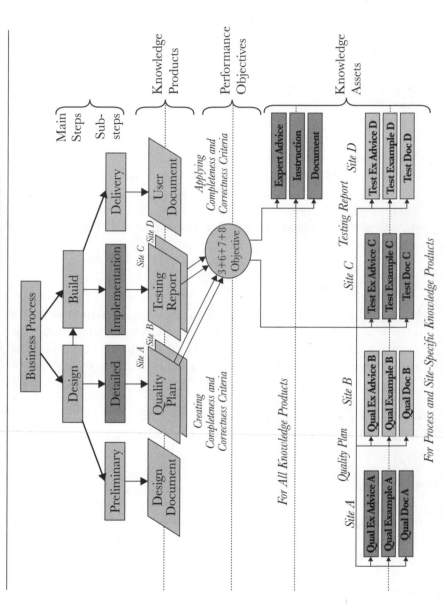

be updated, but Test Doc D and its associated knowledge assets would not.

Of course, the process improvement team will still need a process for deciding whether different knowledge products and different sites are affected by changes in a performance objective, but the point is that the potential impact can now be followed up systematically. By following all the links and inspecting the associated knowledge assets, a process improvement team can ensure that all impacts of making a change in a performance objective are addressed by all possibly affected parties *before* the objective is changed.

To realize innovative learning, an organization must know how its knowledge is organized, how to learn from that knowledge, and how to add this learning to what it knows. Using performance objectives to repurpose knowledge assets provides this important capability.

Application

After reading this section you will be able to describe how to systematically update reused and repurposed knowledge assets in your organization. While you are reading this section you will learn about these two methods:

- How to update reused knowledge assets
- How to update repurposed knowledge assets

How to Update Reused Knowledge Assets

The McBoe process improvement team was quite aware of the main advantage of reusing knowledge assets. For McBoe, updating an objective like Performance Objective 2 & 4 is now straightforward. From a process perspective, if someone can remember all the places in the process and all the sites that can be affected by the proposed changes, then it's simply a matter of resolving any differences among process places and physical sites about what those changes should be. For example, to update Performance Objective 2 & 4, all the process improvement team needs to do is simply send the proposed changes to representatives of the detailed design subprocess workers who develop the quality plan at Sites A and B and the representatives of the implementation subprocess workers who develop the testing report at Sites C and D. Once agreement is made, then—and this was now the easy part for McBoe—simply revise the text in the document that describes the performance objective and it is updated for all users that access that document. McBoe found that these revisions did affect the instruction and the expert advice, so these were also updated. McBoe found that this system of "update in one place and it is updated everywhere" reduced the chance for error during the update process. However, as discussed in the next section, this approach renders great benefits but soon becomes too complicated for a human to remember all the places in the process and all the sites that can be affected by a proposed change.

Relate to Your Organization. Does your organization have some "low-hanging fruit," some obvious places where it can easily reuse knowledge assets without too much tracking? Can your organization easily track each knowledge asset to every place it is referenced in the organization's business process?

How to Update Repurposed Knowledge Assets

As discussed previously, the McBoe process improvement team felt that it could manually keep track of updating knowledge assets that were reused by performance objectives. However, the team knew early on that they could not keep track of updating knowledge assets that were contextual—that is, specific to a particular knowledge product or site. That's why they built the tables shown in Chapter Seventeen describing how knowledge assets are related; the team could use these tables for updating contextual knowledge assets. The following paragraphs describe how the team used the tables to get the job done.

Shortly after completing its work for updating contextual knowledge assets, the McBoe process improvement team was still not certain that all its effort would pay off. Then it received a request from the strategic planning team (McBoe's CEO, chief technology officer (CTO), and marketing director) to "reorient" performance objectives to the Spokane Standards. These standards employ the normal atmospheric conditions in Spokane, Washington—that is, 2,000 feet above sea level, 65 percent average relative humidity, average high temperature of 82°F, with air speeds usually less than five miles per hour. The idea was that purchasers of McBoe's paper airplanes could expect their plane to perform to certain specifications if flown in Spokane. Customers would also be provided with a table showing the differences in performance that they could expect given the normal atmospheric conditions of their location. The strategic planning team thought this would make it much easier for customers to understand these differences for the varying McBoe paper airplane products for their own location.

Given this new strategic directive the McBoe process improvement team looked through the main processes, subprocesses, knowledge products, and performance objectives listed in Table 17.1 and found Performance Objective 3678, which addressed conditions of performance for McBoe products. Next, the McBoe process improvement team located Performance Objective 3678 in Table 17.2, along with its associated knowledge assets. In Document 3678, they found the following common description of Performance Objective 3678:

> State the requirements, criteria, and conditions for the flight distance
> and acrobatic maneuvers of the airplane.

The process improvement team looked at Table 17.2 to locate the knowledge products and sites where Performance Objective 3678 was currently being addressed. Working with representatives from Site A and Site B (responsible for making quality plans) and representatives from Site C and Site D (responsible for making testing reports), the process improvement team rewrote the common description for Performance Objective 3678 to this new common description:

> State the requirements, criteria, and conditions using the Spokane Standard
> for the flight distance and acrobatic maneuvers of the airplane.

Referring back to Table 17.2, the process improvement team reviewed Instruction 3678 to see if it should be updated given the revision of Performance Objective 3678. They determined that the instruction would not have to be changed.

Next the process improvement team turned its attention to the contextual performance objectives that have to be met by the different knowledge products and sites. Using Table 17.2, the process improvement team provided the site representatives with the process document that described the contextual performance objectives for each one's site. That is, the process improvement team provided Site A with Qual Doc 3678A, Site B with Qual Doc 3678B, Site C with Test Doc 3678C, and Site D with Test Doc 3678D. Only the representatives from Sites B and D found they needed to change their site's contextual performance objective in respect to the change in Performance Objective 3678.

The old description for the contextual performance objective for Site B (Qual Doc 3678B) read as follows:

Requirements criteria are to be measured at 9,000 feet above sea level.

Site B representatives changed this contextual performance objective to read:

Requirements criteria are to be measured at 9,000 feet above sea level. Values are to be adjusted and reported to the Spokane Standard.

Representatives of Site B apparently decided that 9,000 feet is still an important altitude to consider in evaluating the performance of a paper airplane. However, to comply with the new company policy, these representatives also decided to report out in the new Spokane Standard. They followed up by updating the other two associated knowledge assets—Qual Ex Advice 3678B and Qual Example 3678B.

For the manufacturing site that decided it needed changes (Site D), the old description for the contextual performance objective (Test Doc 3678D) read as follows:

Requirements criteria are to be measured at the manufacturing site. Measures will be taken within 4 hours after final assembly.

Representatives of Site D apparently recognized that trying to measure the performance of a soggy plane and adjust the values to predict what the plane would do under the Spokane Standard was just too much guesswork. So they decided to change their contextual performance objective to ensure that Site D planes were a little dryer during testing (even if they had to be held in inventory a couple of hours longer). The new contextual performance objective for Site D now read:

> Requirements criteria are to be measured at the manufacturing site. Measures will be taken at least 6 hours after final assembly.

Representatives of Site D followed up by updating the other two associated knowledge assets—Test Ex Advice 3678D and Test Example 3678D.

Relate to Your Organization. Is your organization facing the same complexity problems as the McBoe Company faced in updating its contextual knowledge assets? Does your organization have a systematic way to update performance objectives so that it can trace the impact on its knowledge assets, knowledge products, and business processes?

CHAPTER NINETEEN

DEPLOYING INFORMATION TECHNOLOGIES

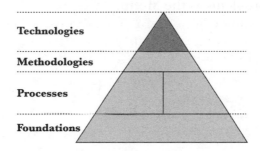

LEARNING OBJECTIVES

After reading this chapter you will be able to do the following:

- *Discuss when* to deploy technologies for managing collaboration, knowledge products, knowledge assets, role-based access, and learning and performance assessment.
- *Describe why* it can be helpful to deploy technologies for managing collaboration, knowledge products, knowledge assets, role-based access, and learning and performance assessment.
- *Describe how* to deploy technologies for managing collaboration, knowledge products, knowledge assets, role-based access, and learning and performance assessment.

Expert Advice

After reading this section you will be able to discuss when to deploy technologies to manage collaboration, knowledge products, knowledge assets, role-based access, and learning and performance assessment.

Dear Mark,

You talk about how organizations create, preserve, and disseminate knowledge. What would the ideal system look like for organizations wishing to take the most advantage of technology for managing their knowledge?

Signed, "Searching for the Ideal System"

Dear "Searching for the Ideal System,"

A few years ago, I had a client who liked to have my firm's design documents printed out on poster paper and mounted in the meeting room for all stakeholders to see. After printing several expensive posters using an outside service, I decided to purchase a high-quality plotter so we could print the posters ourselves. And you guessed it—once purchased it was never used again because by that time our client had gotten used to seeing the design documents on the computer screen. This is an example of investing in technology before identifying the real underlying need.

Designing the ideal system for your organization presents the same problem—you must identify your real needs and not be distracted by available features of technology products. For example, your ideal system will need to support collaboration for creating your knowledge products (design documents, for example) and provide knowledge assets (say, short tutorials) to support and assess the learning needed to create those products. And it will need to provide role-based access to those assets, so that organizational members can drill down and get what they need when they need it.

Remember, begin by defining your collaboration processes, knowledge products, knowledge assets, organizational roles, and learning and performance assessments—then invest in technology that will create the system that meets your real needs.

Concept

After reading this section you will be able to describe why it can be helpful to deploy technologies for managing collaboration, knowledge products, knowledge assets, role-based access, and learning and performance assessment. While you are reading this section you will learn about the following aspects of using technologies to support iLearning:

- Development of a system concept
- Management of collaboration
- Management of knowledge products
- Management of knowledge assets
- Role-based access to knowledge assets
- Assessment of learning and performance

Development of a System Concept

Figure 19.1 provides an overview of a system concept that supports the ongoing life cycle of knowledge in an organization and offers a systemic viewpoint from which to analyze organizational performance problems and to design and implement improvements to resolve those problems.

The lower left-hand corner of Figure 19.1 shows how this system would support collaboration for creating and updating knowledge products and assets. The top middle section of Figure 19.1 is an illustration of the organization's knowledge base, which contains the knowledge products created by the work and the knowledge assets that support the learning needed to do the work. The upper right-hand corner illustrates the different levels of learning and performance assessment—individual, team, and organizational—that the system needs to support. And the lower right-hand corner illustrates the different user roles the system needs to support as well as the varying types of devices that need to be supported.

There are many computer software products that support managing collaboration, knowledge products, knowledge assets, role-based access, and assessment of learning and performance.

FIGURE 19.1. IDEAL SYSTEM CONCEPT.

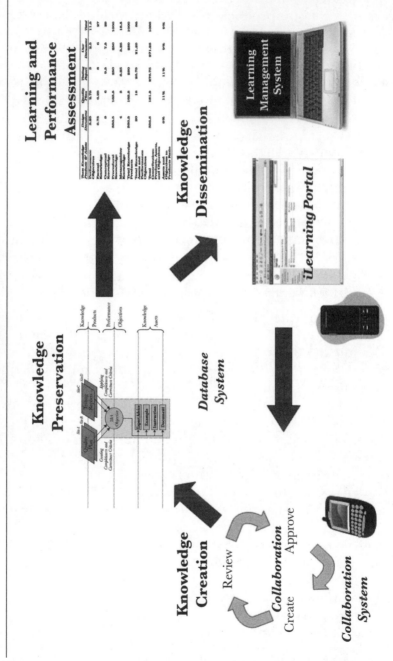

A few of the products of the larger vendors are Novell's Group-Wise; IBM's Lotus product group, which includes Notes, Quick-place, and Sametime; and Microsoft's SharePoint product group, which includes collaboration tools and services, a development platform, and a portal server. These vendors have almost a decade of development in their products, which are now quite seasoned. There are also many smaller vendors that have developed proprietary products—some built from scratch and others built on the products of the larger vendors listed previously. In the last few years other collaboration tools have also joined the scene, such as wikis, blogs, and community spaces. As these technologies mature and become more pervasive, the cost of using them is also plummeting. For example, Microsoft is packaging Share-Point Services 3.0 (a scaled-down version of SharePoint 2007) with Microsoft's Windows Server—making it free of cost with Windows Server. Similarly, Apple provides wikis, blogs, and other collaborative software with its server packages—making them easy to set up and use. Finally, some vendors offer collaboration and management tools as services. For example, Microsoft is planning to offer SharePoint as a hosted service through its partners—entering a crowded field along with Microsoft's own Live Office and Google Sites, which come in free and nearly free varieties depending on how many tools and how much storage space are used.

Even though any single one of these collaboration and management tools may not have all the features needed to support all aspects of iLearning, it will provide plenty of low-cost options for realizing the most important aspects. The trick is, of course, to select and deploy those tools that support the most important aspects of iLearning for a particular organization and to match the technologies in which the organization has already invested.

Management of Collaboration

Apart from choosing among all the available computer software options, the most important aspects of managing collaboration are having a central place in which to work and defining the process for that work. A well-defined and agreed-upon process managed out of a wooden crate will serve you much better than will an ill-defined, controversial process managed by the best software system in the world. And *well defined* doesn't necessarily mean *sequential*. Using a wiki in which all the roles interact at once (authors, reviewers, and approvers) may be the best answer if that is the most efficient and agreed-upon process. (Wikis can be used for more formal, role-based collaborative processes too, but many users are familiar with them from informal processes. And as mentioned in Chapter Three, some organizations may have both informal collaborative processes, where ideas are quickly solidified, and more formal collaborative processes, where changes in the way the organization does its work go through rigorous review and approval.) Having said this, given a well-defined process with agreed-upon rules of engagement (discussed in Chapter Four), technology can aid in supporting that process. One rule of engagement that can be supported with technology concerns the *notification* aspect of the group process. For example, when a new quality plan has been created, the designated plan reviewers can be automatically notified by e-mail or RSS that there is a new quality plan to be reviewed.[1] When all the reviews have been completed, either the person(s) charged with approving the quality plan is notified automatically by e-mail or RSS that there is a new quality plan to be approved or others designated in the process—such as the plan creator—are notified that it has not been approved and requires more (agreed-upon) action. Many computer software products have an automatic *notification* or *alert* capability that sends the right people the right message at the right time in the process. The trick is, of course, to have the right process and rules of engagement in place for the computer software to enforce. Any of the software products that support collaboration and were listed above would do the trick (as would many more that were not listed).

Management of Knowledge Products

Besides providing the notification services just described, computer technology can also assist with managing the history of the artifacts of work—the knowledge products. As described in Chapter Two, the history of knowledge products includes important decisions and rationales that explain why the products look and function as they do. One way computer technology can aid in managing this history is by providing *version control*. This capability allows people involved in the process to focus on the job at hand rather than on creating the *paper trail* that might be needed to understand the work in the future. For example, when a reviewer completes a review of a quality plan, the upload of that reviewed plan, complete with embedded reviewer comments, is automatically treated as a new version of the quality plan. This capability has two benefits for the group. The first is that the new document is denoted as the latest version of the quality plan. The second is that this latest version is placed in proper sequence with the older versions. This version control capability ensures that group members can find and look at the latest version of the group's work; it also puts their previous work in proper context. And version control can be accomplished in a number of ways. Simply working off the most recent page of a wiki is an informal means of version control that can work well for many organizations. Other organizations (or selected processes within a single organization) may need more formal methods for version control, with limited role-based access and archiving features.

Management of Knowledge Assets

The purpose of managing knowledge assets is to make it easy for workers to access them when they are needed (see the Introduction). The main work for accomplishing this goal is to develop a categorization scheme for the organization's intranet so that workers can find things easily. Once this road map to knowledge assets has been created, then computer technology can be applied to manage the assets. One easy way to get started is to create a Web site with an HTML authoring tool (such as Adobe's Dreamweaver or one of a host of other such tools) and then to use the categorization scheme (perhaps the organization's business process, as described in Chapter Three) to organize the site so that members of the organization can drill down and easily find what they need when working a particular task. In the example described in Chapter Three, workers looking for knowledge assets for creating a quality plan could easily drill down and find what they needed. Novices could easily locate instruction, practitioners could easily locate an example, and experts could easily upload expert advice (which could then be easily located by novices and practitioners).

An HTML-created environment can also support the goal of reusing knowledge assets. Each knowledge asset that is accessed from several different places in the process (and perhaps from different locations) can reside in one place on the intranet but be linked to all the places in the road map where members of the organization need to access it. However, as discussed in Chapter Eighteen, managing contextual knowledge assets is a more complex problem than managing other knowledge assets. Careful attention must be paid to the relationships between the knowledge assets, performance objectives, and knowledge products so that when performance objectives change, all the affected knowledge assets can be updated.

The method presented in this book for managing knowledge assets involves drawing up tables to document the relationships among the knowledge assets, performance objectives, and knowledge products. It is possible to do this with pencil and paper. However, managing such well-defined data (entities and their relationships) is what computer technology is really good for. This is a perfect application for a database system. All the collaboration and management tools discussed at the beginning of this chapter employ an underlying database system. This means they can be used to manage knowledge assets in terms of performance objectives. The trick is to make the performance objectives the *center* of the content that is managed. Database fields need to be set up so they mirror the entity and relationship tables outlined in Chapters Fourteen and Seventeen and associate performance objectives with the knowledge assets and context needed to address them. Additionally, when knowledge assets are repurposed and need an update, this method makes search and retrieval an easy task.

Role-Based Access to Knowledge Assets

Knowledge assets can be used for learning and improving performance in two main ways. The more traditional way is to organize knowledge assets into a course and manage that course through a learning management system (LMS). As discussed in Chapter

One, instructional designers have been solving organizational performance problems through the development of courses for decades. This tried-and-true method is more than accepted—it is expected. This means that organizations have to support the taking of courses by workers as preparation for work and support for professional development.

The other way to use knowledge assets for learning and improving performance is to apply the iLearning paradigm presented in this book. Instead of learning before taking on work, workers learn during work and use that learning to spur innovation in that work. In an iLearning organization, collaborative workers need more than access to entire courses on line, they also need access to the right knowledge assets for the right people at the right time. That means collaborative teams need access to an *iLearning portal*—an interface with a database of knowledge assets that displays selected assets appropriate to the profile of the team members—the part of the business process they are working in, the physical site they are working at, and the level of expertise they have for the job at hand (expert, practitioner, or novice).

Most organizations will want to deploy technologies that support both of these ways that knowledge assets can be used for learning and improving performance. The trick, of course, is to use the same knowledge assets for building courses that will reside in an LMS and for populating the database of an iLearning portal. As the lower right-hand side of Figure 19.1 shows, the LMS and the iLearning portal link to the same stored knowledge assets. (Many LMSs have the capability to *pull* in content from a database system.) The LMS provides access to entire courses that students can enroll in, complete, and get credit for. The iLearning portal provides quick and easy access for users at the reusable information object level, where an individual object is a process document, an instruction module, an example, or a piece of expert advice. In an LMS these individual knowledge assets cannot be accessed directly. To get to them students must page through an individual course. And that sums up the difference between the iLearning portal and the LMS. The LMS has all the trappings of a traditional course management (enrollment, assessment, credit, and so on) but lacks direct access to individual chunks of course content. The iLearning portal lacks the trappings of a traditional course but does provide direct access to the individual chunks of course content—providing the right information to the right people at the right time.

Many of the collaboration and management tools discussed earlier have the capability to create a portal for customized access to knowledge assets for designated organizational members. So an organization could create this portal then use the chosen tool further to create a unique profile for each group of its workers. With some further customization, all workers could then use the portal to log on to a Web site with a common area. Then, with some system configuration, the Web site can be customized so that workers automatically go to a common area and from there, as they drill down in the data, be directed to the appropriate knowledge assets for their site and task at hand.

Again, the trick is to use the same knowledge assets for building courses that will reside in an LMS and for populating the iLearning portal database. Obviously, the difficulty in accomplishing this will depend on the LMS and the collaboration and management tool that an organization uses. In some cases the LMS may be able to pull knowledge assets directly out of the collaboration and management tool. In other cases a shared *data store* may have to be created to move shared knowledge assets between the LMS and the collaboration and management tool.

Assessment of Learning and Performance

Chapter Twelve discusses how to use tables to track an individual's contribution to knowledge products and knowledge assets in a collaborative work process where the individual has had the role of author, reviewer, or approver of content. The obvious question is, Where do the data for these tables come from? They could come from records kept by individuals and managers and could be entered into the tables by hand. It doesn't take much contemplation, however, to realize that this manual approach would soon fail miserably. The resulting tables would hold often inaccurate, incomplete, and expensive data that workers and managers would resent collecting. Fortunately, technology is perfect for collecting this type of information and for doing it as the work is going on. It is so much better that it is, in effect, the only way to collect these data. Because all the collaboration and management tools discussed earlier are built on a database, it is an easy operation to tag individual contributions at the time of submittal, by author, type, time, and the like. For example, one individual contribution might be tagged with "Fred," "expert advice," and "January 24, 2008." Then pulling up the expert advice that Fred has contributed on this date is simply a search and retrieval task— "find all expert advice provided by Fred during this time period." A similar database search and retrieval can be used to collect and retrieve information on individual contributions to performance objectives, instruction modules, and examples. The retrieved data for individuals can be consolidated to create a view of team knowledge contributions (see Chapter Thirteen) and also further rolled up to create an organizational view of learning and performance (see Chapter Fourteen).

Application

After reading this section you will be able to describe how to deploy technologies for managing collaboration, knowledge products, knowledge assets, role-based access, and learning and performance assessment. While you are reading this section you will learn about the following aspects of deploying technologies:

- How to design a system concept
- How to manage collaboration
- How to manage the knowledge products of work
- How to manage the knowledge assets for learning
- How to view knowledge assets by role
- How to assess learning and performance

How to Design a System Concept

McBoe's system concept turned out to be a variation of the one shown in Figure 19.1. The center of McBoe's system is the knowledge base for the company. That knowledge base contains not only the knowledge products produced by the company but also the knowledge assets that contain the information for learning to make those knowledge products. To support easy updates of knowledge assets and the variety of user roles, the knowledge base also includes the associations between the elements of the knowledge assets. McBoe's system concept also supports collaboration for creating and updating knowledge assets. This has required configuring McBoe's collaboration and management software to collect data on individual actions while each worker is in the role of author, reviewer, or approver of content for knowledge products and assets. And McBoe's system also supports an LMS and an iLearning portal. The LMS provides courses for McBoe U—a corporate university with features for enrollment, assessment, credit, and so forth but no direct access to individual chunks of course content. The McBoe iLearning portal provides direct access to the individual chunks of course content—providing the right information to the right people at the right time.

Relate to Your Organization. Does your organization need a system concept based on the life cycle of knowledge in the organization? Does it need to provide access to traditional courses through an LMS? Is an iLearning portal needed to provide access to individual chunks of information in a just-in-time manner?

How to Manage Collaboration

McBoe recognized that to improve collaboration it had to make it easy. The problem was that McBoe needed a way to visually model its complex collaboration process. It also needed a way to easily modify and update its process. And finally, it wanted the workers in this collaboration process to be able to perform all their collaboration tasks in one place and to require no or little training on the new collaboration system. In order to meet this challenge, McBoe really focused on the specifics of its collaboration process. It modeled the process with an off-the-shelf flowchart software tool. Then it purchased and installed an off-the-shelf collaboration and management system. Next, it set up its collaboration process in the system. To make the system easy for workers to use, McBoe used the alert feature extensively. The following is a simplified description of one of McBoe's more formal collaboration processes. (McBoe also set up some informal collaboration processes in which all the roles interact at once—authors, reviewers, and approvers—to quickly solidify some ideas for improvements. Then, McBoe used a more formal process to adopt those improvements.)

At the start of this more formal collaboration process, the author of the first draft of a knowledge product uploads it to the *latest draft* area on the Web site of the collaboration system. This sets off an alert that results in an e-mail (McBoe considered sending an RSS but settled on an e-mail) sent to the reviewer and notifying him or her that a new draft of a knowledge product is available. This e-mail also gives the reviewer instructions about placing the reviewed draft on the collaboration Web site. After the reviewer has conducted the review, he or she places the draft knowledge product with the review comments on the collaboration site. If the reviewed knowledge product has no substantial comments to be addressed by the author, the reviewer places it in the *ready for approval* area on the Web site, and an alert generates an e-mail to the approver. If the reviewed product does have substantial comments to be addressed by the author, the reviewer places it in the *needs minor revision* area, and an alert generates an e-mail to the author. If the reviewed product has a major revision to be addressed by the author, the reviewer places it in the *needs major revision* area and an alert generates an e-mail to the author. After the author revises the draft of the knowledge product, he or she places the revised draft in the latest draft area on the collaboration Web site and the process begins all over again. The approver follows steps that are very similar to those of the reviewer. Rejected drafts of a knowledge product go to the *needs revision* area on the collaboration Web site, and approved drafts go to the *released work* area. The latter action triggers another process, this one for collecting examples of work, and an alert generates an e-mail to the author for documenting the example as a new knowledge asset.

McBoe created similar processes to update its knowledge assets—process documents, instruction modules, and expert advice. In each case McBoe focused on the specifics of its collaboration process and used the off-the-shelf flowchart software tool to come to agreement on that process (which was the same for all the knowledge assets). McBoe used technology to enforce its well-thought-out process. Also, the resulting system was used to enforce the rules of engagement that McBoe had developed for its process.

Relate to Your Organization. Does your organization need to improve collaboration and make it easy? Would your organization benefit from modeling its collaboration processes with an off-the-shelf flowchart software tool? Can your organization use standard features, such as the alert feature for notification or an off-the-shelf collaboration system, to enforce its rules of engagement?

How to Manage the Knowledge Products of Work

When McBoe was looking at ways to improve its process for creating a quality plan, it knew that some of the problem with a delay was really about people and how people put things off. As described in Chapter Five, after collecting some metrics, the process improvement team found that the delay was occurring in the review of quality plans. So, the process improvement team struck a deal with the reviewers to send them no more than twenty minutes' worth of work at a time if they promised to turn it around in seventy-two hours. What the team then did was to send the reviewers a module of content that addressed one of the performance objectives for a quality plan.

One of the reasons this approach worked—with the average time needed to review a quality plan dropping from thirty-two days to ten days—was the collaboration system. It was used to manage the correspondence between the process members, and the collaboration Web site was used to store the results. Although each quality plan was broken into modules in order to reduce the overall time needed for reviewing the plan, these modules were stored together. Because each module addressed a performance objective, just a little extra work was needed to regroup the modules into one document for a quality plan.

Relate to Your Organization. Does your organization need to break its knowledge products into modules in order to reduce the time needed to complete the overall collaboration process? Does it have a means to regroup these modules into one document?

How to Manage the Knowledge Assets for Learning

In its first efforts, McBoe did not use a database to manage its knowledge assets. Instead, it tried a simple, HTML-based approach, creating a hierarchy of Web pages organized around the road map for its business process. The initial work went quickly, and the first version of the site was soon operational. This HTML-created environment also supported McBoe's goal of reusing knowledge assets. Identical knowledge assets that were accessed from different places in the process (and from different sites) were simply put in one place on the Web site and then linked to all the places on the road map where workers needed to access them. McBoe's information technology (IT) group did this by hand. This approach turned out to involve a little bit of manual work—but it was certainly manageable.

However, when the network of knowledge assets was expanded to include repurposed contextual knowledge assets (as shown in Figure 18.2), things got quite a bit messier for McBoe. But the process improvement team had done the preparation for this situation when it created the tables (Chapter Fourteen) for updating McBoe's knowledge asset network. The tables provided a systematic way to go about updating performance objectives so that McBoe could trace the impact on knowledge assets, knowledge products, and their business process. All that needed to be done was to automate those tables: that is, put them into a collaboration and management system built on a database system. This collaboration and management system became a *link management* system for McBoe. As team members filled the collaboration and management system with these associations, they knew they were on the right track. There was no way to update these knowledge assets without knowing all these associations between performance objectives, knowledge assets, knowledge products, and the business process.

Relate to Your Organization. Does your organization have a collaboration and management system to track performance objectives that are addressed uniquely in different parts of the business process? How about tracking performance objectives that are addressed uniquely at different sites? Does your organization have the ability to trace changes in performance objectives to the changes needed in the associated knowledge assets?

How to View Knowledge Assets by Role

McBoe created an iLearning portal for its collaboration and management tool. It also decided not to limit people's access to knowledge assets based on their roles. What was most important to McBoe was that when a team was collaboratively working a particular task, the right knowledge assets were readily accessible to all the team members. So, McBoe's iLearning portal directed workers to the knowledge assets they needed whether they accessed those assets from a road map built on McBoe's business process or from a directory that listed McBoe's manufacturing tasks by category. However, McBoe did restrict people's access to its knowledge products based on their roles. For example, once the review phase was complete and a knowledge product was awaiting approval, reviewers could not access the product again and place additional comments in it. McBoe also created an interface to the iLearning portal that could serve up knowledge assets to PDAs and cell phones. That way, for example, workers on a testing site who are writing a testing report could easily access the knowledge assets they needed. Although it looks a little different, the PDA and cell phone interface works like the personal computer interface so that when workers log on to the iLearning portal, they automatically go to the appropriate knowledge assets area for their site, where they can drill down and easily find what they need (at McBoe, of course, these knowledge assets were accessible to workers at other sites too).

Relate to Your Organization. Does your organization need role-based access to knowledge assets? Does it need to make it easy for members of unique groups to access the knowledge assets specific to their group? Does your organization need to allow access to its system through devices such as PDAs or cell phones?

How to Assess Learning and Performance

McBoe used its off-the-shelf collaboration and management system to collect data on individual actions while workers were in the role of author, reviewer, or approver of content for knowledge products and assets. Here is the way McBoe captured the data for Fred, the McBoe employee we first met in Chapter Twelve, with its collaboration and management system. For each quality plan that Fred authored, he filled out a *revision history* identifying the major and minor revisions and the author of each revision. For example, when he first submitted a quality plan it had no revisions. After it was reviewed by John, Fred addressed John's comments and added some text supplied by John. When Fred resubmitted the quality plan, it had a revision history that showed a minor revision contributed by John. The revision history continues to be compiled in this way during the approval process. McBoe decided to capture the author's name, publication date, type of knowledge product, and revision history with metadata in the quality plan document. In looking back at Table 12.1, "Procedural Knowledge Contributed by an Individual," we see that Fred created 40 content modules to address 40 performance objectives. To generate the data found in Table 12.1, a search was performed on the revision history of all the content modules "touched" (authored, reviewed, or approved) by Fred during the completed performance period. Some simple addition revealed that Fred should receive credit for authoring 50 content modules. The same approach was used to gather data to assess Fred's other types of contributions at the individual level—performance objectives, factual knowledge, conceptual knowledge, and metacognitive knowledge—and to assess Fred's total contribution to all knowledge assets (as discussed in Chapter Twelve). To generate the tables describing contributions at the team level, McBoe used a simple spreadsheet for recording the data on individuals, consolidating it, and creating a summary of team knowledge contributions (as shown in Chapter Thirteen, Table 13.1). Finally, McBoe took this team data and rolled it up in a spreadsheet to provide an organizational view of learning and performance (as shown in Chapter Fourteen, Tables 14.2, 14.3, and 14.4).

Relate to Your Organization. Does your organization have procedures in place to tally the total knowledge that an individual contributes to its products and knowledge assets? Does it easily track—or give credit for—the review and approval of other workers' knowledge products and assets? Can your organization easily generate reports that give individuals an insight into how their contribution to the organization's knowledge products and assets affects team and organizational performance?

Note

1. RSS (really simple syndication) is a type of Web feed format used to publish frequently updated content, such as blog entries, news headlines, or podcasts. RSS content is sometimes referred to as a *feed, Web feed,* or *channel,* and it is read with RSS reader software. Individuals and organizations subscribe to an RSS feed by entering the feed's link into the RSS reader. They then check the feed regularly for new content, downloading any new updates.

PART FIVE

FUTURE DIRECTIONS FOR iLEARNING

CHAPTER TWENTY

EMERGING INFORMATION TECHNOLOGIES

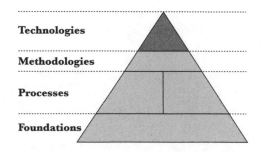

LEARNING OBJECTIVES

After reading this chapter you will be able to do the following:

- *Discuss where* emerging technologies may support iLearning organizations.
- *Describe why* emerging technologies may support iLearning organizations.
- *Describe how* to employ emerging technologies to support iLearning in your organization.

EXPERT ADVICE

After reading this section you will be able to discuss where emerging technologies may support iLearning organizations.

Dear Mark,

I just bought a new cell phone and, wow, I can't believe what this thing can do. It seems that we have just rounded a corner in the development of a new technology. I am not sure about all the ways we can use this technology in our organization, but it sure seems to me that it will change the way we work. What do you think?

Signed, "At the Crossroads of Change"

Dear "At the Crossroads of Change,"

Over twenty years ago, my mentor and adviser at the University of Oregon, David Moursund, used to pose the following question in his doctoral-level seminar. From what I remember, it went something like this: "If people had a portable computing device on their wrist—like a wristwatch—what questions would they ask?"

Students in the seminar called it the Dick Tracy question. (For those who don't remember Dick Tracy, he was a fictional detective who communicated with his fellow crime fighters through the use of a wrist radio.) It was an intriguing question. Remember, this was before the Internet, pocket PCs, cell phones— you get the idea. David Moursund's purpose behind this question was to get people to think about how such access to information would change the way we learn. Now, if you have used any of the new cell phones, you realize that we are on the cusp of answering Moursund's question posed so many years ago. And I believe the answer is not so surprising after all—people want to solve the problem at hand.

Remember, these new portable communication devices are computing devices too. They make it possible for collaborators to see the way problems were solved in the past—knowledge that can be used to better solve problems in the present. And they can make the current best solution available for solving problems in the future.

CONCEPT

After reading this section you will be able to describe why emerging technologies may support iLearning organizations. While you

are reading this section you will learn about the following technological trends:

- Technology is mobile.
- New media forms are available.
- 3-D environments are evolving.

TECHNOLOGY IS MOBILE

It doesn't take much imagination to see cell phones becoming
portable workstations. Maybe you won't wear one on your wrist,
but it will be somewhere on your person, and it will connect you
to the rest of the world. New services will emerge to support these
new workstations. Small foldout keyboards and projector screens
will be available, as will new software services such as *global backup,*
which for a small monthly fee will allow your portable workstation to continually back up its entire content on a remote server.
Now, imagine that you are going golfing and your portable workstation drops on the driveway behind your car as you are loading
your golf clubs. You forget about it until you are backing out of
the driveway. The unmistakable "crunch" reminds you where you
dropped it. You are annoyed but not devastated. You simply swing
by the phone dealer on your way home from golfing and pick up a
new portable workstation. By the time you reach home, it will have
downloaded all your files, and this new portable workstation will
be as ready for you to use as your old one was, before you heard
the crunch.

Your portable workstation will be your communication device
for collaboration, access to knowledge assets, and the contribution
of your expertise to your organization. The emergence of such
portable workstations will greatly accelerate the preponderance of
iLearning—innovating learning in organizations.

NEW MEDIA FORMS ARE AVAILABLE

Traditionally, computer technology has been used to create documents, store them, and retrieve them for further use. As we have

discussed at length in this book, documents are a great medium for creating, capturing, and sharing factual knowledge in organizations. If you want everyone to know a process—then write down the steps in a document. However, newer media forms are now available for supporting the learning that goes on in collaborative organizations. For example, instead of writing a process down in a document, you might capture it in a video clip and then annotate the clip with information about the steps (making the factual knowledge explicit for viewers). Rather than having to recreate the process from words alone, workers who access the clip can now see what the process is as well as hearing it described. These new media forms can also support the life cycles of the other forms of knowledge that iLearning involves. For example, a video clip showing how the wings of an airplane provide lift is much more effective for instruction than a textual description with still pictures. Video showing how to apply the principle of lift to wing design is much more effective than simply describing this application with text and graphics. And finally, a video showing the difference between two or more solutions and explaining when and where each should be used is much more effective than just reading about the difference and looking at pictures. (For an excellent overview of this topic, see Richard Mayer's book, *Multimedia Learning*.[1]) These new media forms give organizations a means to accelerate their iLearning, as workers create, capture, and share knowledge more easily.

3-D Environments Are Evolving

New media forms can accelerate iLearning in organizations, but the emerging 3-D environments, such as Second Life,[2] will move it to a higher level. This will happen because iLearning and 3-D environments are complementary supportive tools for organizations. As Second Life and other emerging 3-D environments become more popular, the features and user interfaces of these tools will become more standardized. On the authoring side, *creation* features, such as the ability to individualize the appearance and gestures of avatars, will be more standardized. And on the user side, the ways of navigating and communicating to others will develop common elements. This means that when new users come to a new interactive learning experience using a 3-D environment, they will already have an idea about how things will work and will be able to focus on the learning experience itself, not on how to navigate and communicate with others. As a result, 3-D environments will greatly accelerate the creation and acceptance of simulated learning experiences in organizational settings.

Taking an iLearning approach to building these learning experiences can greatly simplify the work that goes into them. Typically, simulations are used to teach *cognitive strategies* by taking participants through a scenario where they must make correct choices at the decision points presented to them. Such simulations are also typically *full simulations,* covering the many performance objectives that make up a cognitive strategy. Participants try many options and fail many times—but through this trial and error they learn the correct choices and leave the simulation with a cognitive strategy for solving a similar problem in real life. The idea is to fail in the simulation, learn from it, and be successful in real life.

Using an iLearning approach when developing this type of learning experience is much simpler and more direct than other approaches for two reasons. One reason is that iLearning will focus on *mini-simulations,* and each mini-sim will be simply another knowledge asset. And because it will be related to a single performance objective, it can be much more focused than a full simulation. The second reason is that other knowledge assets will be available during the mini-sim—so if the user does not know the correct action to take, the policy document, the instruction module, an example, and expert advice will be readily available. No extended trial and error is required of the user in order to gain the knowledge needed to take the correct action. In short, the mini-sim is much easier to create than a full simulation—and is much less frustrating for the users.

These emerging 3-D environments may also be employed for role playing in which several participants interact. Say, for example, that a mini-sim for a performance objective that states, "Customer service associates will employ company guidelines when customers return merchandise," has been identified as an important one for new employees. As part of their orientation training, new employees participate with instructors to role-play the correct action to take when following organizational guidelines with a difficult customer. Note that with participants' access to the other knowledge assets, the exercise is short and sweet, and because it is virtual, new employees all over the world can participate. Best of all, the knowledge assets remain accessible for employees later when they are on the job.

APPLICATION

After reading this section you will be able to describe how to employ emerging technologies to support iLearning in your organization. While you are reading this section you will learn how to use three emerging technologies:

- How to use mobile technology to support iLearning
- How to use new media forms to support iLearning
- How to use 3-D environments to support iLearning

HOW TO USE MOBILE TECHNOLOGY TO SUPPORT iLEARNING

By the time you read this book, the McBoe Company will have its portable workstation program well under way. Each worker will have a cell phone that "extends" his or her laptop to give him or her increased learning and collaboration capabilities. As Dorothy in the movie version of the *Wizard of Oz* could go home at any time, workers at McBoe can easily collaborate with others and view knowledge assets at any time. This personal technology has greatly leveraged McBoe's strategy to embrace iLearning to improve organizational learning and performance. For example, just three years ago, McBoe had a *footprint* of twenty working days for creating a quality plan for a new paper airplane. This included authoring the quality plan, reviewing it, and approving the plan. After checking the metrics for this process, the process improvement team reported to the quality plan workers that the approval step actually took up to 50 percent of the total process time. In other words, of the twenty working days needed to develop a quality plan, ten of them were spent waiting on the manager who performed the approvals. In looking into this situation further, the process improvement team found that the manager rarely disapproved a quality plan that had been reviewed and recommended for approval. When the team interviewed the manager, his explanation was simple. He traveled a lot and he didn't always have Internet access. However, with a little more prying, the team found that the manager also felt uncomfortable approving a plan he knew little about. So, when a new quality plan came up for approval while he was traveling, he would wait until he returned to his office. There, he would compare the new quality plan to other recent ones that had been approved. Then he would discuss the new plan with the reviewers who had recommended its approval. Then and only then, would he approve the new quality plan.

The process improvement team recommended that the quality plan workers begin using the new cell phones with Internet access and e-mail capabilities. After that, the footprint for developing quality plans decreased substantially. You guessed it, the traveling manager who approves the plans reduced his time from ten days to four days (he is still pretty busy with other work). Using his new portable workstation, no matter where he is he can access the plans ready for approval, review the policy on plans, skim through the instruction on plans, look at examples of previous plans, and call the people who reviewed the new plans and recommended their approval. The technology provides him with what he needed—access to the different types of knowledge that go into a quality plan. It's a welcome change—but not a surprise. The surprise is that the rest of the process is also shorter owing to the new personal workstations. The workers involved in authoring and reviewing have cut their time from ten days to eight days. The new phones that function like workstations give them access to their work while they are out of the office. Overall, these improvements have reduced the footprint of the quality plan development process—authoring, reviewing, and approving—from twenty days to twelve days. Because time is money, McBoe just saved 40 cents on the dollar with the introduction of the personal workstations.

Relate to Your Organization. Does your organization have a big footprint for a knowledge product owing to delays between the steps in the collaborative process used to create it? Would better communication and access to knowledge assets reduce those delays? Is a personal computing device the answer to improving communication and access to knowledge assets?

How to Use New Media Forms
to Support iLearning

McBoe was once very traditional about how it created, preserved, and disseminated factual knowledge for its manufacturing process. All of McBoe's factual knowledge was captured in process documents, that is, in written text. However, recognizing the value of video for managing factual knowledge, McBoe management decided to use it in the company's new "high-performance best practices" program. The idea behind the program is to capture on video those high-performance workers who are best at certain manufacturing steps. Guess what McBoe is finding out? That's right. When high-performance workers are captured on video, it becomes apparent that they do not follow the current procedures in the process documents.[3] The process improvement team has determined that the procedures of the high performers are more effective in getting the work done. So these new procedures are becoming the current procedures—and the videos of these new procedures are going into the process documents. It has also become apparent that these video documents are more easily followed than the written process documents. Indeed many of the differences between the old and the new procedures are subtle and could not have been clearly communicated in a print document.

McBoe has learned its lesson. It has started to use these new media forms to support the life cycles of the other forms of knowledge in its manufacturing process, and it is now using video for instruction (with video clips showing how the wings of an airplane provide lift and illustrating the performance of different types of wings and how they affect flight). However, McBoe's biggest surprise has been the degree to which the new media forms have supported and encouraged the capture of the other types of knowledge. For example, expert advice was always hard to pin down—especially on paper. It was extremely difficult to get people to set down in writing the best way to approach a particular problem. Now, with a Webcam and recording device, experts can easily and quickly record a couple of minutes of expert advice. A new media form (in this case video) has not only made the process easy but has given the experts a little fame, and that has made all the difference.

Relate to Your Organization. Is your organization aware of the benefits of using new media forms such as video for capturing different types of organizational knowledge? Does it have knowledge that is hard to pin down—especially on paper? Would using a Webcam and recording device make getting that knowledge easier? Would people in your organization provide more knowledge if they were using video and receiving a little fame?

HOW TO USE A 3-D ENVIRONMENT TO SUPPORT iLEARNING

McBoe bought property on Second Life and opened a virtual paper airplane *information center.* Prospective customers can come into the center and look at the airplanes—much as customers do when entering a car dealership in real life. McBoe customer service people represent themselves, as avatars (electronic images), in the Second Life environment. The prospective customers are the avatars of real people interested in paper airplanes. McBoe realized early on that it had to prepare and support its service people if they were to be successful in this new world. It was also clear that there were many similarities between providing good service in Second Life and real life. So, in real iLearning form, McBoe has focused on the knowledge behind the service in order to improve that service. For example, in Second Life as well as real life, customer service representatives will have to deal with a customer who wishes to return a product for the purchase price.

McBoe already knew that good customer service is critical to McBoe's bottom line because the typical customer purchases from twelve to twenty different paper airplanes from McBoe. A well-satisfied customer who has received good customer service will likely buy more McBoe airplanes. So, McBoe wanted to emphasize customer service as part of its orientation training. McBoe instructional designers created a role-playing learning exercise where new employees participate with instructors to achieve the performance objective: "Customer service associates will employ company guidelines when customers return merchandise." After setting up its information center on Second Life, McBoe bought more Second Life property and created a *learning center* exactly like the information center where McBoe customer service representatives—as avatars—would be working. The only difference was that the avatars of real customers would not be able to enter the learning center. McBoe did not want real customers to inadvertently witness learning exercises where instructors—pretending to be avatar customers—were behaving badly. The instructional designers used the Second Life 3-D development environment to create McBoe's learning center. Because most new McBoe customer service employees were familiar with Second Life, they had to spend very little time getting familiar with the learning center. This orientation exercise was quite successful. Participants learned quickly how to deal with difficult customers returning airplanes. More important, participants learned how to locate and apply the knowledge assets that supported the exercise. And they knew where those knowledge assets would be if they later needed to use them with real customers in the McBoe information center on Second Life.

Relate to Your Organization. Does your organization have critical performance objectives that you want new employees to master before they come to work in your organization? Would role-playing learning exercises in a 3-D environment where new employees participate with instructors be an effective way for them to master these objectives? Can knowledge assets be embedded in the role-playing exercise so that these assets are accessible later when the employees are on the job?

Notes
1. R. E. Mayer, *Multimedia Learning* (New York: Cambridge University Press, 2001).
2. Second Life is an Internet-based virtual world developed by Linden Research, Inc. (commonly referred to as Linden Lab) and launched in 2003. It came to international attention via mainstream news media in late 2006 and early 2007; see www.secondlife.com.
3. As noted in Chapter Three, this has already been done by a large manufacturing company. They found that the top performers didn't always follow the "right way" to do a process—providing the basis for a process improvement. For the details see F. Sanchez, "Capturing Expert Knowledge," *Proceedings of the Ninth International Symposium on Semiconductor Manufacturing*, IEEE, 2000, 84–87.

CHAPTER TWENTY-ONE

CHANGING OUR WORLD

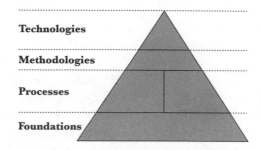

LEARNING OBJECTIVES

After reading this chapter you will be able to do the following:

- *Discuss where* iLearning is changing K–12 schooling, university curriculums, and the global economy.
- *Describe why* iLearning is changing K–12 schooling, university curriculums, and the global economy.
- *Describe how* to anticipate and benefit from the changes in K–12 schooling, university curriculums, and the global economy.

EXPERT ADVICE

After reading this section you will be able to discuss where iLearning is changing K–12 schooling, university curriculums, and the global economy.

Dear Mark,

*I'm a knowledge worker—an individual contributor for a large
semiconductor manufacturer. I have two school-age children. When
I look at what they are learning in school, it scares me. It doesn't seem
to align in any way to what goes on in the work that I do. Do you think
we are on the right course for educating our children for the knowledge
economy?*

Signed, "Concerned for Our Children's Future"

Dear "Concerned for Our Children's Future,"

I recently was a speaker at a meeting where I talked about three major
realizations that will greatly affect the leadership and management of
organizations in the twenty-first century. The first realization is that traditional
learning as we have known it is over. Learning must now be integrated
with work and be continuous. The second realization is that the "Einstein
Approach" doesn't work anymore—we can no longer rely on the brains
of a single genius to solve the problems of our organizations. We must use
our collective brainpower to solve our organizational problems and create
intellectual capital. And the third realization is that our historical means of
measuring individual performance—what people do—doesn't really indicate
the individual's value to his or her organization. The value of knowledge
workers lies in how successful they are in creating, preserving, and applying
knowledge to the problems of their organizations.

Remember, in the knowledge economy, knowledge workers learn while they
work, create knowledge collaboratively, and are evaluated and rewarded by the
knowledge that they create and share. We must ask ourselves if our schools
are preparing our young people to do these things so they can be successful in
the new knowledge economy.

CONCEPT

After reading this section you will be able to describe why iLearning is changing K–12 schooling, university curriculums, and the
global economy. While you are reading this section you will learn
about these changes:

- iLearning is changing K–12 schools.
- iLearning is changing colleges and universities.
- iLearning is changing the global economy.

iLearning Is Changing K–12 Schools

In the light of the evolutionary phenomenon of iLearning, K–12 schools will have to change. How they go about this will depend on the political processes that govern them. But think about it. As it becomes more commonly recognized that adult professionals learn more on the job through work in collaboration with others than they did in school, how can schools not be affected? How can schools continue to have students memorize facts they could easily look up with a portable computing device? How can schools continue to measure what students have learned by giving them individual and isolated tests? Switch this around for a moment. Imagine a large airplane company—one that makes real airplanes, not paper ones—telling its engineering staff, "We want each of you to work alone on identifying possible engineering approaches to a new aircraft. At the end of the week, we will give each of you the requirements for our new aircraft, and working alone, you will have two hours—without consulting any resources—to design an aircraft that meets those requirements." Three things should strike you as obviously wrong. One is why spend all the time up until the end of the week studying engineering approaches one may not use? Two, why work alone on the design—why not work together and get the best design at the earliest possible time? And three, why do the work without consulting any resources—why commit to memory things that could be easily looked up on a computer?

Of course translating current educational practices to a knowledge-intensive work site seems ridiculous. But how about doing it the other way around? Does it make sense to have students learn like knowledge workers? What would that mean? It would mean that students would work in groups to solve authentic problems and would discover how to learn on a just-in-time basis. Projects could include designing and building a bridge, preparing a legal brief, writing a newspaper article that tells the story of the writing of the U.S. Constitution, or building a rocket. Where do all the curriculum materials we already have for K–12 education go, you ask? Why, they are repurposed as knowledge assets to support the completion of these new projects!

iLearning Is Changing Colleges and Universities

iLearning will have an impact on the way institutions of higher education teach their students. The change is already in progress—note the number of online classes offered by colleges and universities. Even though many online offerings are still just traditional classroom courses translated to an online format, changes are beginning to creep in. The college and university programs oriented toward preparing students for employment in corporate settings have been moving toward *group projects* as a means of having students learn how to apply the principles of a discipline to an authentic problem. For example, many undergraduate and graduate programs in computer science have students work in groups on a project for a real client—a company or organization that has agreed to be the customer for a student group project.

This evolution of learning in higher education to look more and more like workplace learning will continue. However, as learning in universities becomes more similar to working in an iLearning organization, a new relationship will emerge between universities and organizations with adult learners. Organizations wishing to accelerate learning and innovation will partner with universities to create new and innovative products based on the latest research. Universities will finally have the ability to infuse new conceptual and metacognitive knowledge into other organizations to greatly shorten product development cycles. Through partnering with organizations, universities will not be out of the loop anymore but rather will be very much a part of new, accelerated loops of innovation.

iLearning Is Changing the Global Economy

iLearning is changing the global economy. For example, a recent article discusses how the Boeing Company is moving to a "collaboration" model of business and away from an "outsourcing" model.[1] The difference is that the first features working and learning together whereas the second tells people, "you do your part and I'll do mine." The 787 airplane project involved over fifty partners from over 130 locations working together over a period of more than four years. From the very beginning, Boeing wanted to work closely with its *partners* (not *suppliers*) and to leverage the learning from collaboration. For example, in the development of composite materials, many being used for the first time, smaller partners developed expertise that was unique. Boeing, acting as a *knowledge broker,* made this expertise available to the other partners who were developing complementary technologies. What this means is that companies are moving away from subcontracting work that is completed with *static knowledge.* Instead, they are adopting a model in which learning is collaborative between partners, and the planned outcomes are innovative products and the knowledge that created them. Old corporate training approaches, where learning is isolated and apart from work, will not achieve these goals. Only innovative organizational learning will provide these new, sought-after results.

APPLICATION

After reading this section, you will be able to describe how to anticipate and benefit from the changes in K–12 schooling, university curriculums, and the global economy. While you are reading this section you will learn about these methods for change.

- How to change K–12 schools with iLearning
- How to change colleges and universities with iLearning
- How to change with the global economy using iLearning

HOW TO CHANGE K–12 SCHOOLS WITH iLEARNING

The McBoe Company is a major employer in the area where its company headquarters is located. As a result the nature of the work at McBoe is known throughout the community. The close relationship between company and community places a lot of pressure on the local public schools to prepare students well for participation in the knowledge economy. Instead of just criticizing these schools, McBoe decided to do something positive about bringing iLearning to the K–12 curriculum.

Several McBoe engineers volunteered to work with the public schools on revamping the curriculum to create an iLearning paradigm in the classroom. McBoe management supported these engineers in this community service activity. To make it a truly collaborative partnership, three McBoe engineers set up a collaboration space and database on a server used for the public schools; these tools were then used for a developing new iLearning curriculum materials. Five sixth-grade math teachers volunteered to participate in the pilot project. These five teachers and the three McBoe engineers then worked collaboratively to create a new student project—designing a new paper airplane! Using the public schools' standards for sixth-grade math, this collaborative team created the problem statement for the knowledge products to be completed by the student project groups. These knowledge products were to be a design document, a quality plan, a testing report, and a user manual—and of course a prototype of the finished paper airplane. The team also created the knowledge assets needed to complete each of the knowledge products. The knowledge assets included a factual description of the performance objectives the student knowledge products would have to meet as well as an instruction module, an example, and some expert advice for meeting the performance objectives. Students used the knowledge assets to work collaboratively to complete their airplane projects. At the end of their projects, students also participated in a collaborative process to add their work (in the form of knowledge assets) to the curriculum for the next batch of students who would be designing a new paper airplane.

Relate to Your Organization. Does your organization have volunteers who are willing to work with K–12 schools in your area? Are there teachers at one of these K–12 schools who would volunteer to participate in a collaborative project with your organization's volunteers? Are there school standards (or goals) for student achievement that can be used to create the problem statement for the knowledge products to be completed by the student project groups?

How to Change Colleges and Universities with iLearning

In this section we'll take a look at a real-life example instead of the generic McBoe Company. In the Organizational Learning and Instructional Technology program at the University of New Mexico, graduate students have worked in groups on student projects for over a decade. These students use educational resources and collaborate with each other to create a solution for a real client's problem. In my courses, students have access to factual knowledge that includes checklists for assignments (telling students *what* to do). They also have access to conceptual knowledge through the texts and assigned readings (telling them *why* to do it) and access to good examples of previous students' work (showing them *how* to do it). And finally, students have access to metacognitive knowledge through lectures and instructor feedback (telling them *when* and *where* to do it). The student teams collaborate on their projects while they have access to these knowledge assets. They also participate in a collaborative process to add their work to the knowledge assets that will be used by the students who will take the course in the following semesters. The idea is to create an iLearning organization in which students collaboratively learn and perform. The goal is not only to prepare students for working and learning in the knowledge economy, but also to maximize their learning while they are at the university.

Most of the graduate students in this program are also employees at area organizations. And many times the projects that they choose are real projects for their organizations, and the work then creates an implied partnership between the university and the organization. As students complete work under the direction of faculty, these projects infuse new knowledge into these organizations and thus provide resources to create innovative products.

Relate to Your Organization. Does your local university have courses that ask students to work collaboratively on projects? Are those projects authentic? Are knowledge assets available for each of the major assignments? Do any of these courses create implied partnerships between the university and other organizations?

How to Change with the Global
Economy Using iLearning

McBoe decided that it wanted to move to a more collaborative business model of with its suppliers and away from an outsourcing model. McBoe's previous history with suppliers was to have them deliver product that met certain requirements set by McBoe. For example, the company that supplies paper for McBoe, Folding Paper Company, was given a list of requirements that the paper would have to meet to be made into a McBoe airplane. These requirements addressed such issues as the length, width, and thickness of the paper and how porous the paper needed be for paint to stick to it properly. They also made it easy for McBoe to compare what other companies would charge for supplying identical paper. Until recently, McBoe management had believed that this buyer-supplier relationship was working very well. Then a manager heard that Folding Paper had developed a new paper product. It was thinner yet stronger than the paper Folding Paper had been supplying to McBoe. It was also shinier—giving it a glossy appearance. When McBoe managers asked Folding Paper why McBoe hadn't been told about this new paper, they got a shock. The people at Folding Paper simply said, "You hadn't asked for it—besides, you seem to be interested only in the price of existing products, not in new products."

That turned out to be a wake-up call for McBoe. It quickly forged a new working relationship with Folding Paper—one in which Folding Paper was a true partner. Folding Paper became an active participant in McBoe's collaborative manufacturing process—especially upstream in the process where design decisions are made before actual materials are chosen. As a full participant, Folding Paper also had access to all the same knowledge assets that McBoe workers used, and participated in the processes to create new and updated assets. McBoe then decided to leverage this learning and make it available to other suppliers who were providing complementary materials, such as the Paint for Paper Company that was supplying the paint for McBoe airplanes. This turned out to be a wise move for McBoe, because the Paint for Paper Company's current line of paint products would not have worked well with the new glossy paper from Folding Paper.

However, by working together and developing complementary paper and paint technologies, McBoe and its new partners introduced a new airplane that took the market by storm. McBoe had moved to a business model in which learning is collaborative between partners and the planned outcomes are innovative airplane products and the knowledge that creates them.

Relate to Your Organization. Does your organization have a history with suppliers in which they simply deliver products that meet certain requirements set by the organization? Are any of these suppliers capable of partnering with your organization to create innovative products? Is it time to move to a model in which learning is collaborative between partners and the planned outcomes are innovative products and the knowledge that creates them?

Note

1. A. MacCormack, T. Forbath, P. Brooks, and P. Kalaher, "Innovation Through Global Collaboration: A New Source of Competitive Advantage," *Harvard Business School (HBS), Working Paper,* July 2007, 07-079.

APPENDIX
iLEARNING RESOURCES

The *iLearning* book Web site (http://www.iLearningU.com) provides the following information and more:

- Podcasts from *The Knowledge Worker* radio show, with the Expert Advice given for each chapter
- Question-and-answer forum with Mark Salisbury, the author of *iLearning*
- Discussion groups for managers of knowledge workers, training professionals, human resource professionals, information technology specialists, and educators
- News about iLearning topics and events
- Information on consulting, training, and software services
- Information on how to become an iLearning partner and services provider

The University of New Mexico's Professional Development Certificate in iLearning Web site offers a PDF (http://www.unm.edu/~olit/ProCerts/Brochures/OLIT_iLearning.pdf) that provides the following information and more:

- Certificate program overview
- Required courses and schedule
- Application procedures

The *iLearning* author Web site (http://www.marksalisbury.com) provides the following information and more:

- Biographical information
- Speaking services

- Consulting services
- Training services
- Software services

The International Society for Performance Improvement (ISPI) Web site (http://www.ispi.org) provides the following information and more:

- Online bookstore (where *iLearning* and other Pfeiffer books can be purchased)
- Link to *iLearning* online contests to win an iPod

INDEX